OECD ECONOMIC SURVEYS

1992-1993

PORTUGAL

ORGANISATION FOR ECONOMIC CO-OPERATION AND DEVELOPMENT

ORGANISATION FOR ECONOMIC CO-OPERATION AND DEVELOPMENT

Pursuant to Article 1 of the Convention signed in Paris on 14th December 1960, and which came into force on 30th September 1961, the Organisation for Economic Co-operation and Development (OECD) shall promote policies designed:

— to achieve the highest sustainable economic growth and employment and a rising standard of living in Member countries, while maintaining financial stability, and thus to contribute to the development of the world economy;

— to contribute to sound economic expansion in Member as well as non-member countries in the process of economic development; and

— to contribute to the expansion of world trade on a multilateral, non-discriminatory basis in accordance with international obligations.

The original Member countries of the OECD are Austria, Belgium, Canada, Denmark, France, Germany, Greece, Iceland, Ireland, Italy, Luxembourg, the Netherlands, Norway, Portugal, Spain, Sweden, Switzerland, Turkey, the United Kingdom and the United States. The following countries became Members subsequently through accession at the dates indicated hereafter: Japan (28th April 1964), Finland (28th January 1969), Australia (7th June 1971) and New Zealand (29th May 1973). The Commission of the European Communities takes part in the work of the OECD (Article 13 of the OECD Convention).

Publié également en français.

Table of contents

Introduction   9

I. The policy implications of the treaty on European Union   11

Introduction   11
The medium-term economic strategy   11
Progress towards convergence   16
Implications of the current policy mix   20

II. Controlling government expenditure   22

The size of government: an international comparison   22
Reforms to improve the control of government expenditure   27

III. Recent economic policies   40

Fiscal policy   40
Monetary and exchange-rate policy   45
Structural policies   53

IV. Recent trends and projections   57

Recent trends   57
The outlook to end-1994   72

V. Conclusions   75

Notes and references   82

Annexes

  I.   Bibliography   84
  II. Supplementary table and diagram   87
 III. Calendar of main economic events   90
 IV. The size of government: some contributory factors   95

Statistical and structural annex   97

Tables

Text

  1. Convergence criteria for EMU and actual performance in 1992   12
  2. The convergence programme for 1992-95 ("Q2") in perspective   15
  3. Financial flows with the EC   20
  4. The size of government: some contributing factors   24
  5. Government expenditure: an international comparison   25
  6. Education in international perspective   26
  7. Composition and growth of government employment   28
  8. Expenditure by lower levels of government   30
  9. Local government accounts   32
 10. Indicators of non-financial public enterprise size and performance   37
 11. Privatisation and the general government borrowing requirement   37
 12. General government account   42
 13. Fiscal stance indicators   45
 14. Money-market intervention and lending rates   47
 15. Recent macroeconomic developments   59
 16. Labour market indicators   61
 17. Wage and price formation   66
 18. Balance of payments   69
 19. The short-term outlook   73

Annexes

Table A1.   Government revenue and expenditure trends   88

Statistical and structural annex

Selected background statistics   99
A.   Expenditure on gross domestic product   100
B.   Household appropriation account   101
C.   General government account   102
D.   Prices and wages   103
E.   Civilian employment by sector   104
F.   Money supply and its counterparts   105
G.   Breakdown by nationality of foreign visitors   106
H.   Foreign trade by main commodity groups   107
I.   Geographical breakdown of foreign trade   108
J.   Balance of payments   109
K.   Labour-market indicators   110
L.   Public sector   111
M.   Production and employment structures   112

Diagrams

1.   The various adjustment programmes   14
2.   Decomposition of changes in the GDP deflator   18
3.   Total and primary government expenditure   23
4.   Pension payments   35
5.   Future public pension expenditure and contributions   36
6.   Adjusted government debt developments   38
7.   Exchange-rate and interest-rate developments   46
8.   Monetary and credit aggregates   49
9.   Interest rates   51
10.   Exchange rate of the escudo *vis-à-vis* selected currencies   54
11.   Evolution of economic performance   58
12.   The labour market   63
13.   Inflation developments   68
14.   Indicators of competitiveness and foreign trade   70

Annexes

Diagram A1.   Welfare payments and beneficiaries   89

BASIC STATISTICS OF PORTUGAL

THE LAND

Area (thousands sq. km)	92.0	Major cities, resident population in thousands (1981):		
		Lisbon		808
		Porto		327

THE PEOPLE

Population (1991, thousands)	9 814	Civilian employment (1991, thousands)	4 607
Number of inhabitants per sq. km	107	As a percentage of total:	
Civilian labour force (1991, thousands)	4 805	Agriculture	17.3
		Industry	34.7
		Services	47.9

PRODUCTION

Gross domestic product in 1991 (million of US dollars)	68 375	Gross domestic product at factor cost by origin (1990, % of total):	
Gross domestic product per head in 1991 (US dollars)	6 967	Agriculture	5.8
		Industry	37.8
Gross fixed asset formation in 1991:		Services	56.4
% of GDP	26.1		
Per head (US dollars)	1 818		

THE GOVERNMENT

Public consumption (1991, % of GDP)	17.2	Composition of Parliament (number of seats):	
Public investment (1991, % of GDP)	3.6	Social Democrats (PSD)	135
(% of total investment)	13.9	Socialists (PS)	72
General Goverment current revenue		Unified Democratic Coalition (CDU)	17
(1991, % of GDP)	38.5	Center Social Democrats (CDS)	5
		National Solidarity (PSN)	1

FOREIGN TRADE

Exports of goods and services (1991, % of GDP)	31.9	Imports of goods and services (1991, % of GDP)	41.3
Main exports as a % of commodities exports, 1991 SITC:		Main imports as a % of commodities imports, 1991 SITC:	
Food, beverages and tobacco (0,1)	7.3	Food, beverages and tobacco (0,1)	11.2
Basic and semi-finished materials (2,3,4)	10.5	Basic and semi-finished materials (2,3,4)	14.5
Manufactured goods (5,6,7,8)	81.9	Manufactured goods (5,6,7,8)	74.2
of which: Chemicals (5)	4.6	*of which:* Chemicals (5)	9.0
Machinery and transport equipment (7)	19.7	Machinery and transport equipment (7)	36.5

THE CURRENCY

Monetary unit: Escudo		Currency units per US $, average of daily figures:	
		Year 1992	134.82
		April 1993	148.59

Note: An international comparison of certain basic statistics is given in an annex table.

This Survey is based on the Secretariat's study prepared for the annual review of Portugal by the Economic and Development Review Committee on 22nd March 1993.

•

After revisions in the light of discussions during the review, final approval of the Survey for publication was given by the Committee on 20th April 1993.

•

The previous Survey of Portugal was issued in January 1992.

Introduction

After several years of strong growth, output expansion slowed to 1½ per cent of GDP in 1992. While domestic demand growth appears to have remained very buoyant until mid-1992, the contribution of the foreign balance to GDP growth was strongly negative, as in 1991. Rapid GDP growth in earlier years had pushed up capacity utilisation rates to very high levels and the unemployment rate down to close to 4 per cent in 1992. The overheating of the economy led to a surge in wage and price inflation between 1989 and 1991. The cooling off in 1992 and falling import prices induced lower wage and price inflation, but underlying inflation has remained stubbornly high (at around 10 per cent adjusted for the effects of increased VAT) and disinflation has largely taken place in the open sector. The current account, however, has swung to balance, reflecting terms-of-trade gains and increasing inflows of EC transfers.

The deepening of macroeconomic imbalances since the late 1980s largely reflect an unbalanced policy stance, with budgetary policy strongly expansionary in 1990 and to a lesser extent in 1991. Hence, monetary policy had to bear the brunt of disinflation. Interest rates rose in nominal and real terms and the exchange rate even appreciated in nominal terms from 1989 until the escudo entered the Exchange Rate Mechanism of the European Monetary System in April 1992. To correct increasing macroeconomic imbalances, the Government announced a medium-term convergence plan in 1991, aimed at a sharp reduction in inflation rates and a considerable cut in the government deficit by 1995. The 1992 Budget was restrictive, largely because of another increase in taxation. New budgeting procedures were able to halt the rise in the expenditure-to-GDP ratio and the government deficit fell to close to 5 per cent of GDP. The 1993 Budget aims at a further fall in the deficit, with expenditure budgeted to expand considerably less than GDP.

Output growth may slow further to just 1 per cent in 1993, as the economy adjusts to a more sustainable course in an environment of weak foreign markets. Some pick-up in growth is foreseen for 1994 as a European-wide recovery takes hold, but slack in goods and labour markets should reduce wage and price inflation further. However, the inflation differential with the EC average might still remain substantial (of the order of 2½ percentage points), and continued restrictive policies will be necessary in order to achieve nominal convergence with the best performing EC countries.

Part I of this Survey reviews macroeconomic policies in a medium-term context, emphasising the need for a better policy mix in order to achieve nominal convergence with other EC countries. Part II analyses government expenditure trends, reforms to control them over recent years and the allocation of public spending across different levels of government. Macroeconomic and structural policies are discussed in Part III, followed by a review of recent trends and the presentation of the OECD projections for 1993 and 1994 in Part IV. Part V draws conclusions.

I. The policy implications of the treaty on European Union

Introduction

The EC integration process since 1986 has encouraged the Portuguese authorities to pursue a number of structural reforms with a view to improving economic performance. The recent acceleration of the integration process and Portugal's commitment to participate in it fully have reinforced the need for adjustment. Since 1986, great progress has been achieved in restructuring the economy. However, two important and related shortcomings must be overcome in the macroeconomic domain in order for Portugal to join the planned European Economic and Monetary Union (EMU): the resilience of inflationary pressures and the persistence of large government deficits.

Indeed, despite recent progress, Portugal is still far from fulfilling the criteria laid out in the Maastricht Treaty, except for the public debt/GDP ratio. The biggest adjustments are needed in inflation and interest rates. While the target for reduction in the government deficit seems to be of a more manageable size, it is crucial that fast progress is made in order to achieve the other objectives (Table 1). This chapter describes and assesses the medium-term economic strategy of the Portuguese Government, discusses the major reasons for the persistence of high inflation and budget deficits in recent years, and highlights the need to follow through on planned changes in the policy mix.

The medium-term economic strategy

The ultimate policy objective is convergence of real per capita income towards average EC levels through steady non-inflationary growth. Since 1987, the Authorities have embarked upon successive medium-term adjustment pro-

Table 1. Convergence criteria for EMU and actual performance in 1992

	Inflation[1]	Divergence[2]	Interest rates (long-term)[3]	Divergence[4]	Deficit to GDP ratio	Divergence	Debt to GDP ratio	Divergence
	(a)	(b)	(c)	(d)	(e)	(f)	(g)	(h)
EMU criteria					3.0		60.0	
Performance in 1992								
Portugal	**8.9**	**6.6**	**15.5**[5]	**6.6**	**5.4**	**2.4**	**64.5**	**4.5**
France	2.8	0.3	9.1	0.1	2.8	-0.2	50.1	-9.9
Germany	4.0	1.6	7.9	-1.0	3.5	0.5	47.7	-12.3
Italy	5.1	2.7	11.5	2.6	11.1	8.1	108.4	48.4
United Kingdom	3.7	1.3	9.1	0.2	6.6	3.6	41.9	-18.1
Spain	5.9	3.5	12.5	3.6	4.7	1.7	48.4	-11.6
Netherlands	3.7	1.2	8.3	-0.6	3.8	0.8	78.3	18.3
Belgium	2.4	0	8.7	-0.2	6.1	3.1	134.4	74.4
Denmark	2.1	-0.3	9.0	0.1	2.6	-0.4	62.2	2.2
Greece	15.9	13.5	26.0	17.1	13.2	10.2	84.3	24.3
Ireland	3.1	0.7	8.7	-0.2	2.5	-0.5	98.1	38.1
Luxembourg	3.2	0.7	8.7	-0.2	0.4	-2.6	6.8	-53.2

1. Consumer-price inflation within 1½ percentage points of the three lowest inflation countries.
2. Inflation (column a) minus unweighted average of inflation in the three lowest inflation countries.
3. Within 2 percentage points of rates in the three lowest inflation countries.
4. Long-term interest rate (column c) minus unweighted average of long-term interest rates in the three lowest inflation countries.
5. Short-term interest rate.

Note: Government deficits and debt refer to consolidated general-government deficits and gross debt. Countries also must have stayed within narrow ERM bands and not have initiated a devaluation within the two previous years.

Sources: OECD, *National Accounts* and *Main Economic Indicators*; OECD estimates; Maastricht Agreement on Economic and Monetary Union.

grammes, each setting out policy objectives and intermediate targets, for a variety of macroeconomic goals (Diagram 1). While growth performance was remarkable until recently, each programme failed to curb inflation sufficiently and, in 1990 and 1991, budget deficits widened again:

- The 1987 Programme for the structural adjustment of the external deficit and unemployment (PCEDED) aimed at redressing main macroeconomic imbalances – large public-sector and current-account deficits and high unemployment – by 1990. Inflation, targeted to fall to 4 per cent by 1989, was not then considered a major problem. While growth was stronger than projected, the rate of inflation turned out some 8½ percentage points above target in 1989.
- A revised version of PCEDED (P2, July 1989) set much less ambitious targets for inflation, the budget deficit and the current account.
- The new schedule for achieving economic and monetary union within the EC and a disappointing inflation performance led to the adoption of still another adjustment plan, the QUANTUM (*Quadro de Ajustamento Nacional para a Transição para a União Economica e Monetaria*, July 1990). With a view to achieving the necessary disinflation to enter the exchange-rate mechanism (ERM) of the EMS, QUANTUM embodied fiscal consolidation through expenditure restraint and an increase in indirect taxes. However, fiscal policy remained procyclical in 1991, contributing to intensifying inflationary pressures.

In November 1991, the Government adopted a convergence programme for 1992-95 (dubbed ''Q2''). According to the programme, Portugal will meet all the requirements for fully participating in EMU by 1995, while output growth is projected to remain above the EC average (Table 2).

As the reduction of inflation is crucial to a sustainable catch-up process, ''Q2'' aims at the virtual elimination of the substantial inflation differential *vis-à-vis* the EC average[1] by 1995. With Portugal's accesion to the exchange rate mechanism (ERM) of the European Monetary System (EMS) in April 1992, the exchange rate became the primary intermediate target of monetary policy. Under ''Q2'', the general-government budget deficit would be halved to 3 per cent of GDP – the Maastricht Treaty target – lowering the public-debt/GDP ratio to 53 per cent at the end of 1995. In contrast to earlier medium-term programmes,

Diagram 1. **THE VARIOUS ADJUSTMENT PROGRAMMES**
Annual growth rates

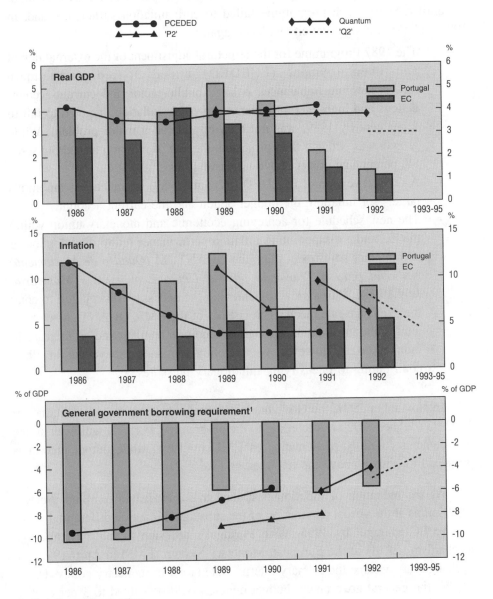

1. Excluding public enterprises.
Sources: Ministry of Finance, "A Strategy of Sustained Regime Change"; OECD, *National Accounts* and estimates.

Table 2. **The convergence programme for 1992-95 ("Q2") in perspective**

Annual percentage changes

	Outcome		"Q2"	
	1986-89	1990-91	1992	1993-95
Demand and output				
Gross domestic product	4.7	3.4	3	3
(Differential *vis-à-vis* EC average)	(1.6)	(1.2)	(1)	(1)
Private consumption	5.1	5.0	3¼	5
Public consumption	5.1	3.3	¾	¾
Gross fixed capital formation	11.7	4.9	7½	5
Exports	10.4	6.5	2	3¾
Imports	16.9	8.6	3¾	4¼
Price deflators				
Gross domestic product	14.1	13.7	10½	4½
Private consumption	10.3	12.4	9¼	4½
(Differential *vis-à-vis* EC average)	(6.8)	(7.7)	(5)	(0)
Public consumption	14.8	18.9	13	5¾
Gross fixed capital formation	11.9	10.6	7½	4½
Exports	8.5	3.9	3¾	3¾
Imports	4.7	4.3	3½	3¾
General government[1]				
Overall balance (excluding financial assets)	−6.9	−5.9	−4	−3
Primary balance[2]	1.4	2.3	5	2
Public debt	71.2	66.3	59	53
Current account balance[1]	0.8	−0.6	−1	−1¾

1. Per cent of GDP.
2. Excluding debt-interest payments.
Sources: Ministry of Finance and OECD *National Accounts.*

the authorities have set precise limits on the level of overall primary expenditure for both the central and the general government. These limits, which are to be invariant to actual inflation outcomes, are compulsory for the State Budget and indicative for the other levels of government, including social security. Wage moderation, greater job flexibility and a reduction in overmanning in the public sector are key elements in the strict control of public spending. Any deviation from voted primary expenditure should call for corrective measures (according to a "non-accommodation principle"); and households' direct-tax brackets and allowances are to be adjusted by no more than the annual target rates of inflation.

"Q2" also calls for reform of the capital, labour and non-tradeable goods markets, featuring prominently the continuation of the privatisation programme. In line with EC directives, the number of public monopolies will be reduced and liberalisation of the communication sector and other services pursued. Furthermore, with the completion of the European Single Market Programme, goods and services markets will be increasingly open to international competition. Deregulation and liberalisation of financial markets will include additional privatisation of the remaining state-owned financial institutions, opening markets to foreign operators and the removal of remaining barriers to the free movement of capital.

Progress towards convergence

Real convergence. Progress towards real economic convergence has made a good start. Real GDP growth turned out to be higher than anticipated by the authorities in each year between 1987-90, and was on average 1.4 percentage points above the EC's. The gap between Portugal's GDP per capita and the EC average in purchasing-parity terms has narrowed from 50 per cent in 1985 to 44 per cent in 1991. At the same time, unemployment fell rapidly, and labour-market performance was among the best in the OECD. For the near-term future, the OECD projections for real GDP growth ($1\frac{1}{4}$ per cent on average in 1992-94) are much less favourable than the official projections made in 1991 and embodied in "Q2" (3 per cent on average in 1992-95). Being close to the projected EC average, they imply limited progress in real convergence during the adjustment period.

Reducing inflation. Despite moderation since 1991, inflation remains a major policy concern. Since 1987, the targets set in the convergence programmes have underestimated inflation by an average of $3\frac{1}{4}$ percentage points a year. Furthermore, the inflation differential with the EC average, which had shrunk to 6 percentage points between 1983 and 1988, widened again to 7.3 points at the end of 1990.[2] Since then, the inflation differential has resumed a steady downward trend, but was still above 4 percentage points at the end of 1992 and $6\frac{1}{2}$ points as compared to the three best-performing EC countries. A number of factors have kept inflation at high levels.

Since EC accession, massive net inflows of private capital and EC transfers ($7\frac{1}{2}$ and $3\frac{1}{4}$ per cent of GDP a year on average in 1989-92, respectively) have strengthened domestic demand, accentuating inflationary pressures. Labour-cost pressures have intensified since about 1989, when the fall in unemployment to very low levels boosted wage claims. High business profits allowed firms to accommodate wage claims, and effective wage increases significantly outstripped collective wage agreements (Diagram 2). High public sector wage increases may also have strengthened wage claims in the private sector. Overall, unit labour costs rose on average by 13 per cent a year in 1987-91.

Fiscal policy also exacerbated inflation. The authorities embarked upon a three-year civil servants' pay-scale reform (October 1989), added a fourteenth month to pension payments in 1990 and increased health benefits in 1991. The public-sector wage reform alone is estimated to have directly added about 3 points to the rise in the GDP deflator over the three years to 1992 (Diagram 2). Even more important, these measures fed already-buoyant domestic demand, as budget deficits widened in an expansionary phase of the cycle. In 1992, the stance of fiscal policy became clearly restrictive, due notably to the reform of the VAT system in line with EC-tax harmonisation. However, with the average VAT rate estimated to have gone up by 2 percentage points, the reform increased prices.

Monetary policy has borne the brunt of the fight against inflation. The monetary authorities considerably tightened monetary conditions in 1989. Reflecting a string of restrictive measures, nominal interest rates rose in the period 1989-91, edging down slowly in the second quarter of 1992. However, the authorities were quickly faced with conflicting objectives typical of an unbalanced policy mix. The interest-differential *vis-à-vis* foreign credit markets widened markedly, stimulating capital inflows from abroad. Temporary restrictions placed on certain types of capital inflows proved unable to neutralise the pull exercised by both high domestic interest rates and the high marginal efficiency of capital in the business sector.

Recognising that the crawling-peg regime was adversely affecting the goal of lowering inflation, the authorities decided to allow the escudo to float in October 1990. With investors attracted by high interest rates and direct investment opportunities in Portugal, the escudo appreciated by 7 per cent[3] in effective terms from the Autumn of 1990 to the end of 1992. Owing to the 10¾ point cumulative inflation differential, the real appreciation was close to 18 per cent. While exchange-rate appreciation dampened inflation, it affected mainly the open

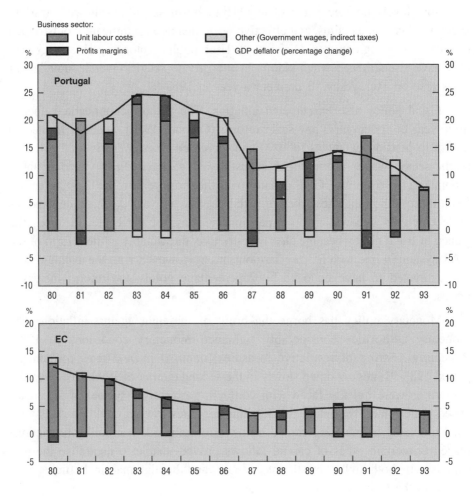

Diagram 2. **DECOMPOSITION OF CHANGES IN THE GDP DEFLATOR**
Contributions in percentage points

Business sector:

Unit labour costs

Other (Government wages, indirect taxes)

Profits margins

GDP deflator (percentage change)

Portugal

EC

Source: OECD.

sector, where profit margins were squeezed. At just under 12 per cent by the end of 1992, underlying inflation has remained stubbornly high (see below). The Government nevertheless judged that progress on the inflation front was sufficient for the escudo to join the ERM of the EMS with a fluctuation band of 6 per cent, which it did in April 1992.

Cutting the government budget deficit. As judged relative to announced policy objectives, meeting budget deficit targets has proved relatively successful, insofar as they have been reached or even overshot since the mid-1980s. However, with hindsight, the 1990 and 1991 targets were not ambitious enough. After improving considerably up until 1989, the general-government deficit increased again in 1990 and 1991 before falling back to an estimated 5 per cent of GDP in 1992. Although the improvement between the mid- and late 1980s was helped by strong growth, discretionary policy changes were even more important for the more than halving of the deficit between 1985 and 1989. In 1990 and 1991, fiscal policy became procyclical, and, at 7 per cent of GDP, the structural deficit was as large in 1991 as it had been in 1985. The estimated improvement in the deficit at a time of relatively sluggish growth points to a considerable tightening of fiscal policy in 1992.

Until 1992, budget consolidation efforts have been concentrated on the revenue side, with the share of government receipts in GDP increasing by 5 percentage points between 1985 and 1992 (Annex II, Table A1). Wide-ranging tax reforms aimed at enhancing tax revenues and the harmonisation of the tax system with that of other EC countries started in 1986. Tax reform was implemented in two major stages. The VAT was introduced in 1986, the year Portugal joined the European Community, and direct taxation of both personal and corporate income was reformed in 1989. The VAT rate structure was adjusted in 1992. As a result, the overall tax burden, which had remained at around 35½ per cent of GDP in the period 1989-91 – about 1 point above its level in 1986-88 – increased to 38.5 per cent in 1992.

In addition to the increase in fiscal pressure, meeting budget-deficit targets was facilitated by EC transfers and privatisation receipts. Transfers from the EC have risen rapidly since 1986, gross and net transfers reaching 4.6 and 3.3 per cent of GDP in 1992, respectively (Table 3). About 80 per cent of total transfers received were EC structural funds and funds under the special programme to assist the Portuguese industry (PEDIP). Transfers are primarily designed to promote infrastructure investment, while smaller amounts are allocated towards training programmes and private investment subsidies. The large inflows have softened the Government's budget constraint and helped to balance the foreign

Table 3. **Financial flows with the EC**

	1986	1988	1990	1991	1992[1]	1993[2]
	Billions escudos					
Payments	41	70	95	127	146	148
Financial contribution	31	36	63	89	108	110
Customs and agricultural levelling duties	10	24	28	38	38	38
Other payments	–	10	4	–	–	–
Receipts	67	168	216	358	524	579
Reimbursement and other receipts	23	25	15	7	2	1
Agricultural guarantee fund	5	27	38	57	84	108
Structural funds	39	108	145	274	417	4 623
PEDIP	–	8	18	20	21	8
Net flow	26	98	121	231	378	431
	Per cent of GDP					
Net flow	0.6	1.6	1.4	2.3	3.3	3.5
Gross inflow	1.5	2.8	2.9	3.6	4.6	4.7
of which: Structural funds and PEDIP	0.9	1.9	1.9	3.0	3.9	3.8

1. Budget estimate.
2. Budget projection.
3. Excludes likely increases due to Cohesion Fund payments.
Source: Ministry of Finance.

account. By increasing demand, they may also have fuelled inflation in an already overheating economy. Thus, while helping achieve real convergence in the long term, they appear to have slowed nominal convergence in recent years (Gaspar and Pereira, 1992).

Implications of the current policy mix

Despite the progress made in 1992, inflation (including rent) and the government deficit are higher now than in the late 1980s. The Government did not take up the opportunity to build on what it had achieved up to 1989 to reduce macroeconomic imbalances further in 1990 and 1991. The relatively lax fiscal policy stance and an increasing emphasis on monetary instruments to control inflation had several important implications. Domestic demand has remained strong and labour market tensions have increased. Monetary restraint has resulted in interest rates that are among the highest in the OECD area. Even so, growth of credit has not slowed sufficiently yet. Furthermore, continuing strong wage increases and a strong currency have negatively affected competitiveness. Relative unit labour costs in manufacturing have increased by a cumulated 28 per cent since 1989, contributing, in combination with strong domestic demand, to a sizeable negative swing in the real foreign balance. For new investment, however, labour cost competitiveness may play little role, as labour cost levels are still much lower than the EC average.

Financial markets viewed the escudo as a devaluation candidate during the ERM-wide financial market turmoil in the autumn of 1992. The monetary authorities have shown great commitment to avoiding a devaluation and they weathered the September storm. But when pressure mounted again in November, they had little choice but to adjust the central parity of the escudo when the peseta was devalued for the second time in just two months. As the change within the grid was limited, the nominal effective exchange rate has barely moved.

This episode should not jeopardise the Government's policy of reducing inflation. Indeed, the Government has announced its intention of maintaining a stable exchange rate. The sustainability of this policy will depend even more on tight budgetary control following the removal of remaining controls on capital outflows at the end of 1992. With activity clearly weaker than projected earlier, meeting fiscal targets in terms of deficit and spending ceilings will probably moderate domestic demand, thereby contributing to further disinflation. The cost of disinflation will largely depend on the response of wages to increasing labour market slack. Portugal's past record is encouraging in this respect.

II. Controlling government expenditure

Expenditure control has become the centerpiece of the Government's new strategy to reduce the budget deficit. Expenditure growth has been rapid in recent years, despite several earlier reforms aimed at a better use of government resources. More recently, the Government enacted a reform of budgeting procedures, proposed some changes to local government activities and opened negotiations on reforming the health-care system. Finally, the Government started to privatise the large State-owned enterprise sector in 1989 in order to improve its efficiency. Privatisation proceeds are earmarked for public debt repayment, thereby reducing interest payments on the public debt.

While the budget deficit was the major fiscal target in earlier adjustment programmes, a spending target (excluding interest payments) has been added in "Q2", the new convergence programme. This spending target, which is set in nominal terms, is binding for the State and indicative for other levels of government. The targets for 1993 are increases of 7.8 and 9.3 per cent for the State and the whole public sector, respectively (compared with an officially projected nominal GDP growth of 10½ per cent). At least for the State, any spending overruns need to be counterbalanced by cuts in other expenditure. Control of the the social security system, the National Health Service and of local authorities has not been changed.

The size of government: an international comparison

In the early 1960s, **total government spending** – comprising central government, local authorities, autonomous regions and social security outlays – was one of the lowest in the OECD area in relation to GDP. Indeed, it was lower only in Switzerland and Japan. The relative size of government has more than doubled since then, reaching 46.1 per cent of GDP in 1992 (Diagram 3), some 5 percent-

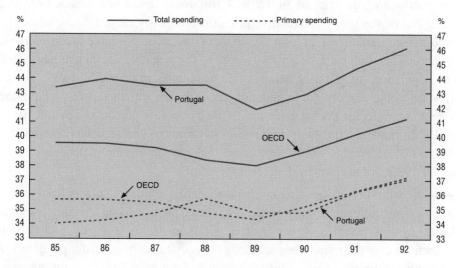

Diagram 3. **TOTAL AND PRIMARY GOVERNMENT EXPENDITURE**
Per cent of GDP

Source: OECD.

age points higher than the OECD average. Excluding interest payments, however, the expenditure ratio was considerably lower: at 37.1 per cent it was close to the OECD average. On this basis, the public sector does not appear to be larger than elsewhere, but the trend increase in primary expenditure, which has continued in recent years, is disquieting.

It is difficult to judge whether public expenditure shares are high or low by international comparison, as the factors affecting demand for, and supply of, public goods differ across countries. In order to shed some light on this question, cross-country regressions of the share of primary expenditure in GDP (measured in Purchasing Power Parities – PPPs) against various determinants of demand and supply were estimated for 19 OECD countries (for a similar exercise, see Schultze, 1992). The independent variables are demographic factors (the shares of the population below 15 years and above 65 years in total population), population size, population density and the relative price of government consumption as measured in PPP's (PPP's for total government expenditure are not available). The data are averages for the 1970s and 1980s, stacked together for

23

the purpose of running a pooled time series and cross-section regression. Regression results are summarised in Table 4 (for more detail see Annex IV). The coefficient of the proxy for relative price differences is close to one, while the demographic variables – at least the share of the elderly – have a considerable impact on spending patterns across countries. The negative coefficient associated with population suggests substantial scale economies in providing public goods, offset by some penalty for population density. The equation overpredicts the expenditure ratio for Portugal for the 1970s by some 4 percentage points. Since the 1970s, however, the sharp increase in government spending has changed the situation considerably, with the equation underpredicting the expenditure share for the 1980s somewhat (by 1 percentage point).

Comparability of spending components across countries suffers from differences in institutional arrangements. For instance, spending by the National Health System (roughly 4 per cent of GDP in 1990) is partly included in government consumption, while it belongs to social security transfer payments in many other countries. Even after taking such differences into account, **government consumption,** measured in PPPs, appears to be relatively high (Table 5). *Per capita* government consumption was only 25 per cent lower than the OECD average, while *per capita* GDP was 50 per cent lower.[4]

The share of **government investment,** on the other hand, is not much higher than in many other OECD countries and has not risen significantly up to 1991 despite the increase in EC trends to finance the development of infrastructure

Table 4. **The size of government: some contributing factors**

	Primary expenditure to GDP ratio	
Relative price effect	0.96	(12.6)
Population	−0.08	(−5.7)
Population above 65 years	0.65	(4.3)
Population below 15 years	0.05	(0.3)
Population density	0.06	(3.9)
R2	0.90	
S.E.E.	0.11	

Note: All data are in logs. T-statistics are in parentheses.
Source: OECD estimates.

Table 5.   **Government expenditure: an international comparison**

A. Government consumption (1990)

	Per cent of GDP		Per capita[1]	
	National prices	International prices	National prices	International prices
Portugal	**16.7**[2]	**23.3**[2]	**34**	**75**
United States	18.2	15.2	125	119
Japan	9.0	10.3	69	67
France	18.0	18.5	123	118
Sweden	27.8	28.4	240	177
Netherlands	14.7	16.0	90	92
Austria	17.9	18.5	118	112
Spain	15.2[2]	19.0[2]	62	82
Total OECD	16.0	16.0	100	100

B. Other expenditure (1992)

	Transfers	Subsidies	Investment
	Per cent of GDP		
Portugal	**13.0**	**1.4**	**4.2**
United States	14.4	0.0	..
Japan	11.9	0.4	5.4
France	24.2	1.4	3.3
Sweden	25.4	6.7	2.4
Netherlands	28.3	2.6	2.2
Austria	20.6	2.9	3.1
Spain	17.7	1.6	5.0

1. Index relative to OECD average.
2. A large part of public health expenditure is included in government consumption.
Sources: OECD (1990), *Purchasing Power Parities and Real Expenditure,* and Ministry of Finance.

since 1986.[5] (Table 5 and Annex II, Table A1). Going directly to private enter-prises, however, part of the EC funds have been used to upgrade human capital via education and training. In 1992, Portugal's government investment in per cent of GDP was lower than in Spain, where it has grown rapidly.

Public spending on **education** (partly included in government consumption, partly in investment) has advanced fast, reflecting increasing numbers of teaching personnel and schools. As a per cent of GDP, however, spending is still lagging behind the more advanced OECD economies (Table 6). School enrolment rates have risen rapidly in the higher secondary and tertiary sectors, but are still

Table 6. Education in international perspective

Per cent

	Portugal	USA	Japan	France	Sweden	Netherlands	Austria	Spain
Expenditure on education[1]								
Total	**4.9**	5.7	4.9	5.7	5.7	6.6	5.6	5.0
Public	**4.7**	5.0	3.8	5.1	5.7	6.3	5.6	3.9
Expenditure per student[2]								
Relative to GDP per head	**23.7**	22.0	22.8	23.1	32.7	27.5	27.9	19.2
Enrolled persons in education[3]	**44.2**	54.9	57.2	62.0	48.5	58.2	51.0	59.6
Educational attainment[4]								
Primary and pre-primary	**89**	8	..	24	..	19	..	67
Lower secondary	**4**	10	30	26	33	26	35	13
Higher secondary	**2**	46	48	33	44	36	60	10
Tertiary and other[5]	**6**	35	21	14	23	19	5	9

1. Per cent of GDP, excluding private expenditure in Austria.
2. Public expenditure only for the United States (*i.e.* excluding high private spending on higher education).
3. Per cent of population aged 2-29, full-time equivalent.
4. Per cent of the population 25 to 64 years of age, 1989 (1990 for the Netherlands). In Portugal and Spain, the expansion of secondary education, which has occurred relatively recently is not yet reflected in the data.
5. University and non-university. In France, 3 per cent of the relevant population is in "other education".

Source: OECD (1992), *Education at a glance.*

considerably lower than elsewhere in the OECD. While the number of pupils in primary education has started to fall, the strong rise in expenditure on higher education is likely to continue, investment in human capital being a priority spending area of the government. Educational attainment of the population as a whole is still low, reflecting the earlier lack of concern for investment in human capital.

Public transfers remain low relative to GDP, at least if compared to many other European countries. As noted above, most health expenditure is not channelled through the social security system, which explains part of the difference. In addition, good labour-market performance and low levels of spending on labour-market programmes have also contributed to relatively low spending on transfers. Demographic factors, on the other hand, have evolved roughly in line with other countries. Since the mid-1980s, the Government has reduced its involvement in the business sector, so that transfers to business have become less important.

Reforms to improve the control of government expenditure

Administrative reform

Since 1987 various steps have been taken aiming at a stricter monitoring of the growth and a better allocation of resources. The programme of the new Government, approved in 1991, again stressed the need for improved responsiveness by the public administration, emphasising the possibilities of improving the quality of service and for the rationalisation of structures and procedures. To this end a commission, which reports to the Secretary of State for Administrative Modernisation, has been created. Its task is to carry out a qualitative and quantitative analysis of the public sector and to recommend initiatives which would improve service level and decrease costs. It should identify activities suitable for privatisation and forms and mechanisms for implementation.

In the domain of budgeting procedures, the earlier system of *a priori* monitoring of expenditure is gradually being phased out. It gave little financial autonomy to public services in the use of funds and led to delays in decision-making due to complex administrative procedures. The new *a posteriori* control system gives autonomy to departments in the allocation of voted expenditure.

Under the new procedures, accounting is based upon commitments. Complemented by cost-accounting, these rules strengthen the control of public spending. Transactions of the Funds and Autonomous Servcies, which are all included in the State Budget, have been put upon an accrual basis. In addition, a new electronic payment system set up in June 1992 centralizes information about personnel and purchase management as well as about the inventory system. According to a recent EC study (Jurgen von Hagen, 1992), budgeting procedures strongly influence the achievement of fiscal targets. Ranking EC countries' budgeting procedures in 1990 according to various criteria, Portugal came out rather poorly. While the new procedures are certainly an improvement, it is too early to judge their effectiveness.

Already during the 1980s, measures had been designed to monitor the qualifications of civil servants prior to recruitment, to upgrade the skills of officials and to enhance departmental and geographic mobility. As a result, the composition of public employment has changed considerably since 1979 (Table 7). The number of higher qualified officials increased much faster than that of lower qualified ones. However, containing the increase in the number of government officials proved to be less successful. While central-government employment increased less between 1986 and 1991 than in earlier periods, it still

Table 7. **Composition and growth of government employment**

	1979	1986	1988	1991
A. Structure of employment				
Share of employees with				
higher education	44.1	51.9	53.8	..
secondary education	55.9	48.1	46.2	..
B. Employment (thousands)				
Total employment	..	520	544	624
(Per cent of aggregate employment)	..	(12.8)	(12.7)	(13.5)
Local government	..	80	80	81
Social security administration	..	21	20	21
Health	..	101	107	123
Education	..	187	210	247
Other	..	131	127	152

Source: Ministry of Finance.

rose by an average annual rate of close to 3 per cent. Local government employment, on the other hand, was virtually stable. Measures to increase the scope for employment flexibility for civil servants were taken in October 1992: the definition of redundant employment was extended to include jobs affected by the disappearance of government services and entities and by changes in required qualifications. Officials holding posts which have been suppressed are now placed in a central pool, either receiving training and being offered another job with the government, or taking advantage of early retirement, or leaving with an indemnity. People in the pool will see their salaries gradually decline to 60 per cent over a 3-year period. Greater flexibility will, indeed, be needed in order to achieve the volume cuts in central government consumption announced in the 1993 Budget (see below).

Pay scales for officials, which are also binding for employees of local governments and the social security schemes, were modified in 1989 in order to allow the Government to offer wages better attuned to the labour market. The new wage scales exhibit a much wider dispersion than the earlier ones and are closer to private-sector wages. There are special scales for the health, education and research sectors. The effect of this reform on the government's wage bill was rather dramatic and lasted until 1992. Wages per government employee outstripped private-sector pay-increases by a cumulated 15 per cent between 1989 and 1992 and the share of government consumption in GDP increased markedly.

Despite the reform efforts, the terms of public employment and remuneration packages are still rigid: short-term contracts and contracts under private sector conditions are virtually non-existent. Transfer of employees between the public and private sectors is not encouraged. Finally, pay-scales are not linked to performance and are the same for central and local governments and autonomous funds and, therefore, independent of local labour market conditions and work effort. Rigid wage-setting procedures in the public sector are certainly not peculiar to the Portuguese administration; they can be observed in many OECD countries (Katz and Krueger, 1992).

Reform of local government

The government aims at a devolution of responsibilities to local authorities in order to improve resource allocation overall and give citizens a better choice in the provision of locally provided public goods and services. In Portugal, as would be expected in a unitary state, the share of local government in government spending (excluding social security) is small. It is, in fact, extremely small, even for a unitary state (Table 8). The minor role played by local government can be related to the size of the country with a rather homogeneous population in lingual, racial and religious terms. Up to the mid-1970s political factors certainly also played a role. As public issues were decided in Lisbon, this may have contributed to a concentration of resources there and to a fairly uneven regional development (Cohn and Costa, 1986).

While local government outlays increased rapidly in recent years, their share in GDP was only 4.3 per cent in 1991 (Table 9), reflecting the limited responsibilities held by municipalities. They include minor tasks in the areas of education, health and social housing. Local authorities have full responsibilities for town-planning and municipal cultural and sports facilities, waste disposal, water supply, civil protection, transport infrastructure and regulation of some commercial activities (for instance, administration of markets). For the City of Lisbon, which in many respects may not be representative, but which accounted for about 12 per cent of total municipal spending, the largest expenditure items are related to housing, transport infrastructure and waste disposal. The limited degree of involvement in such areas as education, health and public security is shown by the fact that municipal spending on these items together was about as large as that on the municipal fire-brigades. Municipalities have little influence on deci-

Table 8. **Expenditure by lower levels of government**

Per cent of total expenditure, excluding social security

	1980	1990
Portugal	**10.8**	**10.0**
Germany	65.6	61.4
France	25.9	22.3
Austria	42.9	38.7
Belgium	22.1	18.2
Netherlands	50.5	43.0
Spain	..	39.0[1]
Sweden	50.4	49.6

1. 1989.
Sources: OECD, *National Accounts* and Ministry of Finance.

sions about the number of hospital beds, schools or policemen in their area and cannot rectify any perceived imbalances as their fund-raising powers are also limited.

While autonomous in their financial decisions, municipalities have to respect strict budgetary rules: current expenditure ought not to exceed current receipts, and expenditure on wages three quarters of current receipts of the previous year. Medium- and long-term borrowing is only permitted for investment purposes, and local government debt is small (amounting to 1 per cent of total government debt in 1991). Local government receipts include local taxes, transfers from higher levels of government and revenues from user charges (Table 9). Local direct taxes stem largely from property taxes and a surcharge on business taxes (up to a maximum rate of 10 per cent); indirect taxes are related to VAT receipts from tourism. Together, they represented 26 per cent of local revenues in 1991. Another 10 per cent of revenues comes from user charges. The latter are estimated to cover only about 60 per cent of the cost of services on average.

Transfers from the State budget, which are based upon projected VAT receipts and calculated according to a formula (including population, area size, dwellings, fiscal receipts per capita and basic needs) accounted for about 35 per cent of local government receipts in 1991. Until 1991, population size accounted for 45 per cent of global central government transfers, and other criteria, including the length of the road network, area size and the number of parishes, for about 40 per cent. This points to a significant redistributive effect of transfers across municipalities (Pinto Barbosa, 1992). The sharp increase in EC transfers has largely offset the fall in the share of central government transfers. It has, in addition, not translated into an equally sharp acceleration in local authority investment spending.

While the Government is strongly committed to a devolution of tasks to local authorities, this process has just started. Current proposals amount to a very limited agenda: the right of the local authorities to administer the level of public support to private institutions undertaking social work in their jurisdiction; the decentralisation of social support related to education; and the transfer of collection of local taxes – so far centralised – to municipalities. More could be done to give local citizens a greater choice in the supply of local public goods. It is difficult, however, to find optimal solutions as equity and efficiency considera-

Table 9. **Local government accounts**

	Receipts	
	Per cent of total receipts	
	1987	1991
Taxes	24.2	25.9
Charges and property income	10.2	10.2
Current transfers[1]	28.3	21.1
Other receipts	4.0	2.2
Total current receipts	66.7	59.4
Capital transfers		
FEF[1]	18.8	14.1
Community Funds	3.7	11.6
Other	3.5	4.5
Other capital receipts	7.2	10.4
Total capital receipts	33.2	40.6
Total receipts	100.0	100.0

	Outlays	
	Per cent of total outlays	
	1987	1991
Personnel	29.0	29.1
Goods and services	14.7	14.2
Debt-interest payments	2.9	2.8
Other current expenditure	7.7	7.1
Total current expenditure	54.3	53.1
Investment	38.9	39.1
Other capital expenditure	6.8	7.8
Total capital outlays	45.7	46.9
Total expenditure	100.0	100.0

1. From the State budget.
Source: Ministry of Planning, *Finanças Municipais.*

tions may clash and decentralisation may have a cost. While there is typically a desire to improve living standards in lagging regions, for instance, the social rate of return on infrastructure investment in richer agglomerations may be higher. There may also be economies of scale in providing public goods, which could make decentralised provision more expensive (Owen, 1989). Also the shift of responsibilities to lower levels of government needs to be managed with care:

administration at the central level should be reduced as well as central government taxation and there needs to be a clear delimitation of competences.

Reform of the welfare system

The welfare system in Portugal comprises the social-security system (largely transfer payments), the National Health Service (mainly included in government consumption) and welfare payments to civil servants (included in the government's wage bill). The social-security system is financed by employers' and employees' contributions as well as from transfers from the State budget, the National Health Service largely by central government transfers, and government pensions by general government receipts and by employers' and employees'contributions. All welfare payments together, as measured by the European Integrated Statistics System for Social Welfare, increased by $1\frac{1}{2}$ percentage points to 16 per cent of GDP between 1985 and 1990. Social-security transfer payments, as measured by the National Accounts, increased by $1\frac{3}{4}$ percentage points between 1985 and 1992. The rapid rise in total welfare payments comes against the background of a large fall in the unemployment rate, from 8.5 per cent in 1985 to close to 4 per cent in 1992.

Health expenditure rose broadly in line with GDP between 1985 and 1990, averaging 3.8 per cent of GDP (Annex II, Diagram A1). This situation is likely to have changed in the last two years, reflecting the impact of the Government's public-sector pay reform and the increase in the number of health professionals in the National Health Service from 88 000 in 1985 to 102 000 in 1991. For 1991, the Ministry of Finance estimated an increase in outlays on personnel and goods and services of 30 and 25 per cent, respectively. Excluding investment-related items, Government transfers to the National Health Service also grew rapidly.

The public health-care system is likely to run a large deficit in 1993. In order to avoid another surge in transfer payments, the Government has opened negotiations in order to rein in future cost pressures. These negotiations are at an early stage. A proposal by the Health Ministry features prominently the establishment of an alternative private system. Users with a private insurance contract would choose between public and private health facilities and private insurance companies would need to participate in the funding of the public health infrastructure. In addition, management of some public hospitals could be handed over to private insurers, with doctors working for both systems. The Government would

33

fund about two-thirds of total health expenditure in the future, the rest coming from private insurance. It is difficult to judge the outcome of the current negotiations at this stage. It is clear, however, that the ageing of the population and improved health technology has put quite some pressure on health expenditure elsewhere and reforms were only partially successful in containing cost pressure.

Spending on **disability pensions,** which may partly serve as a substitute for unemployment benefits, and over which monitoring was lax in the past, has increased only slowly in recent years. The Government has tightened the monitoring of applicants for invalidity pensions and sickness benefits; and health checks of the former have been transferred to social security from the National Health Service. The number of beneficiaries has been declining steadily since 1989.

While not on the official agenda, the old-age **pension system** may need reform. Old-age pension payments have increased fastest among the different welfare programmes, while the number of beneficiaries has changed little (Annex II, Diagram A1). As in most other OECD countries, higher life expectancy and smaller cohorts to support the elderly in the next century are likely to increase tax and spending pressures considerably. The Portuguese pension system is very similar to that in other European countries. Financing is on a pay-as-you-go basis, existing pensions are usually adjusted to inflation, and new pensions levels depend on the best 5 years of earnings received over the last 10 years of contribution to the social-security system. Since the mid-1980s, spending on old-age pensions has far outstripped inflation and real wage gains (Diagram 4). The sharp increase in spending per beneficiary reflects improved generosity (a fourteenth month of pension payments was added) and a structural shift from low pensions in agriculture to higher pensions in the non-agricultural sector. Due to favourable demographic developments and strong revenue growth, it has been possible so far to finance the social-security system without an increase in contribution rates.

Over the next decade, the financial position of the social-security system may not change much, as still favourable demographic developments and strong real wage growth could lead to fast revenue increases. However, assuming constant contribution rates, eligibility criteria and indexation of pensions to price developments, Borges and Lucena (1988) found that the deficit of the social security system (pensions, family allowances and spending related to the labour

Diagram 4. **PENSION PAYMENTS**

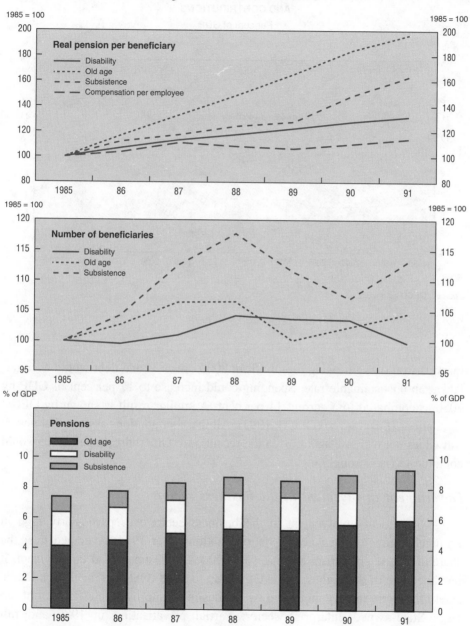

1985 = 100

Real pension per beneficiary

—— Disability
······ Old age
– – – Subsistence
— — Compensation per employee

1985 = 100

1985   86   87   88   89   90   91

1985 = 100

Number of beneficiaries

—— Disability
······ Old age
– – – Subsistence

1985 = 100

1985   86   87   88   89   90   91

% of GDP

Pensions

■ Old age
□ Disability
▨ Subsistence

% of GDP

1985   86   87   88   89   90   91

Source: National Institute of Statistics, 1991, *Statistical Yearbook.*

35

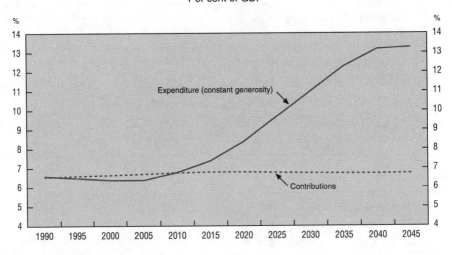

Diagram 5. **FUTURE PUBLIC PENSION EXPENDITURE
AND CONTRIBUTIONS**
Per cent of GDP

Source: OECD estimates.

market) would begin rising rapidly from 2000 onwards and debt would accumu-
late at an unsustainable rate. Spending could increase to 17 per cent of GDP by
2050 as compared to a current 11 per cent. A similar result is shown by OECD
simulations (Diagram 5) (OECD, 1993). All these simulations assume that generosity does not increase as fast as in the recent past. Otherwise, expenditure would
continue to rise strongly.

Government involvement in the business sector

Government involvement in the business sector was particularly high in
Portugal following the wave of nationalisations after 1974. Averaged over the
share of public enterprises in total value added, investment and employment, it
remained one of the highest in the OECD up to 1988 (Oxley *et al.*, 1991). Public
asset sales were largely motivated by the desire to improve the efficiency of the
large State-owned enterprise sector. Partial privatisation in 1989 and full
privatisation since 1990 has led to a significant fall in government involvement in
the financial and non-financial sector. Employment in public enterprises fell by

Table 10. **Indicators of non-financial public enterprise size and performance**

	1989	1990	1991
Shares in economy-wide data (per cent)			
Value added	12.4	11.2	10.7
Investment	15.5	15.2	14.8
Employment	3.8	3.4	2.9
Non-financial public enterprises (Esc. billion)			
Subsidies and capital transfers	261	72	52
Cash flow	155	209	226
Own capital	922	1 472	1 469

Source: Ministry of Finance.

close to a cumulated 15 per cent between 1988 and 1992 (Table 10). The fall was steepest in the industrial and financial sector, with little change occurring so far in the communications sector. However, the State plans to retain a majority in certain privatised enterprises. Moreover, the current policy of limiting foreign investors' ownership on a case-by-case basis appears to violate EC competition rules.

Privatisation has also significantly reduced the need to finance ailing public enterprises. According to GAFEEP estimates (Ministry of Finance, 1992), subsidies and capital increases provided by the state amounted to Esc 2 361 billion between 1978 and 1991 (equivalent to 24 per cent of GDP in 1991). Government

Table 11. **Privatisation and the general government borrowing requirement**
Per cent of GDP

	1988	1989	1990	1991	1992[1]	1993[1]
Budget deficit	5.7	3.4	5.5	6.4	4.9	4.0
Privatisation receipts	..	−0.6	−1.2	−0.9	−2.6	−1.8
Other operations[2]	3.4	3.2	2.0	0.2	2.6	1.2
General government borrowing requirement	9.3	5.9	6.2	5.7	4.8	3.4

1. Budget estimates.
2. Debt take-over, capital increases for public enterprises, accounting adjustment.
Sources: Bank of Portugal, and Budget estimates, Ministry of Finance.

receipts in terms of corporate taxes and dividends, on the other hand, were negligible. Subsidy payments and capital increases have fallen in recent years, while the cash-flow situation of public enterprises has improved and the own capital base increased.

As privatisation receipts are earmarked for retiring government debt, privatisation has influenced debt accumulation directly, thereby reducing future interest payments. Since 1989 28 enterprises have been privatised, yielding receipts of Esc 677 billion (6½ per cent of 1992 GDP). The State received Esc 506 billion, non-State shareholders Esc 60 billion, and Esc 112 billion were used to fund capital increases. In the reorganising of public enterprises the State took over large amounts of their debt. Such debt take-overs have been of decreasing significance (Table 11). On the other hand, the Government's policy of using

Diagram 6. **ADJUSTED GOVERNMENT DEBT DEVELOPMENTS**[1]

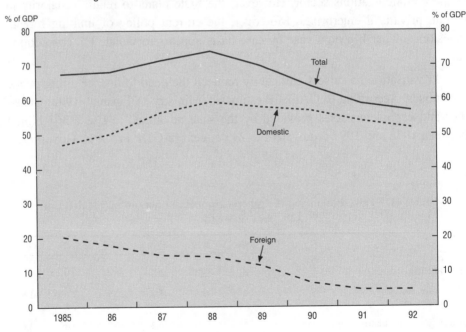

1. Adjusted for Treasury bills used by the Central Bank between 1991 and mid-1992 for purposes of liquidity absorption.
Source: Ministry of Finance.

privatisation proceeds to reduce government debt has become more important, and the adjusted public-debt-to-GDP ratio, after reaching a peak of 74 per cent in 1988, has fallen back to close to 60 per cent in 1992 (Diagram 6). Current plans continue to focus on privatisation of financial and industrial enterprises, while privatisation of public utilities in the energy sector and in communications, though not ruled out in principle, is not on the agenda yet.

In sum, attempts to rein in pressure on public spending have proved difficult in recent years. While the reform of the large State-owned enterprise sector has considerably reduced aid to ailing enterprises and privatisation receipts have damped debt accumulation, government consumption and transfer expenditure to households have advanced rapidly. Investments in human and infrastructure capital will remain priority spending areas and, in order to allow increases in real terms, volume cuts in other areas are unavoidable. Such cuts are envisaged for the State in 1993 and will put the Government's commitment to reach the budget target to a serious test. Apart from the State, spending pressure might increase considerably for pensions and health expenditure in the medium term. In addition, devolution of responsibilities to local authorities may not be costless.

III.   Recent economic policies

Until 1992, policy geared towards inflation control was based mainly on a tightening of monetary conditions, which, in the absence of comparable restraint in the fiscal domain, led to high real and nominal interest rates. The exchange rate appreciated considerably in real terms despite controls on capital inflows, resulting in a diversion of strong domestic demand to imports. Since the tightening stance of monetary policy was not accompanied by an equally tight fiscal policy, economic policy had little success in slowing down domestic spending. This changed in 1992. A renewed emphasis on expenditure control and tax increases led to a restrictive 1992 Budget, and a further cut in the deficit is foreseen for 1993. Policy also aims at wage moderation in the context of an economy-wide incomes accord. The improved policy mix, anchored in the government's medium-term convergence programme, a downward trend in inflation and the projected slowdown in domestic demand justified the participation of the escudo in the ERM as of April 1992, and remaining capital controls were lifted later in the year. The stability of the exchange rate is now the primary intermediate target of monetary policy. The resolve of the monetary authorities to defend the escudo's parity has already been put to the test during the turmoil in financial markets in the autumn of 1992. The escudo was devalued relative to the strongest EMS currencies, but only reluctantly, and in the context of other parity adjustments. This chapter reviews macroeconomic policies and structural policy initiatives.

Fiscal policy

The 1992 Budget and estimated outturn

In line with ''Q2'', the new convergence programme, the Government has aimed at a nominal spending target, excluding debt-interest payments, since the

1992 Budget, in addition to achieving a certain deficit level. The target – which is binding for the State and indicative for other government entities – was set at Esc 2.7 trilion for the State and Esc 4.6 trillion for the public sector as a whole. The general government deficit (on a public accounts basis) was projected to fall from 6.4 per cent of GDP in 1991 to 5.2 per cent in 1992. The 1992 spending target aimed at stabilising the expenditure-to-GDP ratio, the deficit reduction being largely achieved by increasing the tax burden further. Official estimates for 1992 suggest that budgetary outcomes were broadly in line with fiscal targets. Current receipts and expenditure have been higher, counterbalanced by lower receipts and spending on the capital account.

Indirect taxes increased steeply in 1992, reflecting harmonisation of the Portuguese tax code with EC initiatives (Table 12). Goods and services which benefited from a zero-rating are now taxed at 5 per cent, the Community's minimum rate. On the other hand, goods previously taxed at 8 per cent are now taxed at either the minimum rate or the standard rate, which was lowered by 1 percentage point, to 16 per cent. The standard rate is 1 per cent above the Community's minimum standard rate. Excise taxes were also changed signifi-cantly. Direct tax brackets and tax allowances and deductions were raised by 8 per cent, the mid-point of the Government's 1992 target range for inflation. With incomes increasing at an estimated 16 per cent, fiscal drag and continuing strong corporate tax receipts boosted direct tax receipts, which rose by more than 20 per cent.

Spending on goods and services expanded by close to 15 per cent in 1992. The government wage and pension bill was boosted by the lagged effects of the government's multi-year pay scale reform discussed above, while public-sector wage scales were adjusted by 8.8 per cent. Transfer payments increased by an estimated 10.5 per cent, above the Budget forecast, which was about in line with the inflation objective. A rapid increase was recorded for interest expenditure, reflecting the strong increase in the public sector borrowing requirement and the Central Bank's continued use of Treasury bills for the conduct of monetary policy. The latter led to both a rise in interest expenditure and property income receipts.[6] Capital expenditure is likely to rise significantly less than budgeted. While spending on investment should remain strong, capital transfers could be much lower, in line with lower capital receipts.

Table 12. **General government account**

Public accounts basis

	1991 Outcome	1992 Budget figures	1992 Estimate [1]	1993 Budget figures
	Billion escudos	Per cent rate of growth		
Current receipts	4 070	15.6	16.6	7.8
Direct taxes	1 040	22.3	23.5	8.7
Social contributions	855	11.5	13.0	10.8
Indirect taxes	1 427	26.9	22.1	10.3
Other	747	−10.7	0.7	−3.8
Current expenditure	4 236	13.8	15.2	4.4
Goods and services	2 059	12.9	14.6	9.2
Subsidies	176	15.5	7.7	15.2
Interest on public debt	840	25.2	22.7	−6.8
Current transfers	1 161	6.7	12.0	3.1
Capital receipts	258	57.9	52.2	1.4
Capital expenditure	691	27.7	21.5	12.0
Investment	395	26.7	24.9	8.4
Capital transfers and other	296	29.1	16.9	17.3
Overall balance [2]	−597	−590	−581	−525
Per cent of GDP	−6.0	−5.2	−5.1	−4.2
Memorandum items:				
Non-interest expenditure	4 086	13.8	14.7	8.3
Primary balance [3]	2.5	4.0	4.0	3.5
Total borrowing requirement [3,4]	−6.5	−5.6	−5.4	−4.6
Public debt [3]	66.7	64.5	64.5	..
Nominal GDP [5]	16.1	13½	14¾	10½

1. Ministry of Finance estimate.
2. Billion escudos.
3. Per cent of GDP.
4. Including financial operations related to public enterprises.
5. Per cent rate of growth.
Sources: Ministry of Finance and Bank of Portugal.

The 1993 Budget

The 1993 Budget, based upon projections of output growth of 3 per cent and a rise in the GDP deflator of 7¼ per cent, aims at reducing the overall deficit to 4.2 per cent of GDP. This is broadly in line with the medium-term convergence plan, which envisages an average budget deficit of 3 per cent of GDP over the 1993 to 1995 period. The deficit is expected to fall by 1 percentage point of GDP compared to the estimated 1992 outcome and would have been lower (close to 3½ per cent), had indirect tax collection not been delayed by the introduction of the Single Market.[7]

This is the second budget based on the non-accommodation principle, implying a binding ceiling on non-interest expenditure in nominal terms of Esc 3.1 trillion for the State and Esc 5.3 trillion for the general government on average between 1993 and 1995. For 1993, current non-interest expenditure is budgeted to increase by 7.8 per cent (to Esc 2.9 trillion) and 8.3 per cent (to Esc 5.1 trillion) for the State and general government, respectively. In 1994 and 1995, nominal primary expenditure will be allowed to increase by about 4½ per cent per year, roughly in line with the official inflation forecast. Higher than expected inflation should lead to very restrictive budgets. For 1993, the expenditure ceiling implies no change in real terms for the State and some increase for the general government but a fall in non-interest expenditure as a share of GDP for both (the latter being projected officially to rise by 10½ per cent). Government consumption for all levels of government is budgeted to increase by nearly 10 per cent, allowing for a small increase in real terms. The limited rise in total current transfer payments reflects a fall in spending on labour-market measures due to more vigorous screening of beneficiaries, fewer invalidity pension recipients, and no increase in transfers to the EC. There is not only a tight constraint on non-interest expenditure, but also interest payments could fall by 7 per cent if interest rates decline by the 2 percentage points projected by the authorities. The retirement of Treasury bills – earlier used by the Central Bank in its conduct of monetary policy – is also contributing to lowering interest payments.[8] In total, general government expenditure is projected to fall by 2 percentage points in relation to GDP.

For the State, spending on transfers and investment expenditure is being increased by nearly 10 per cent, but government consumption will rise by only 7.3 per cent, considerably less than for the whole public sector. With the changes in budgeting procedures, this year's State Budget estimates for consumption are based on volume changes from last year, while a general contingency reserve has been voted for the Finance Ministry, which will be used in part to pay for wage increases. For 1993, a cut in volume of 2.4 per cent is envisaged: apart from the Ministries of Justice and the Interior, which will have their expenditure increased slightly on a volume basis, all other Ministries will have to cut substantially. The largest cuts are foreseen in the Finance Ministry (18 per cent), while they will be of an order of magnitude of about 5 per cent in the other Ministries, except for education, where a minor reduction is envisaged. In the meantime government wage scales have been adjusted by 5 per cent and somewhat more for low-wage earners. Including wage drift, compensation (including pension payments) for all levels of government is likely to increase by 9½ per cent. If volume is cut as planned, total government consumption will increase in nominal terms as budgeted.

Total revenues are projected by the authorities to increase somewhat more than expenditure, but still less than GDP. The sluggish revenue increase is due partly to a fall in property income, but also to the delay in indirect tax collection due to the start of the Single Market. Tax brackets, deductions and allowances have been raised by 6 per cent in line with the Government's target for consumer-price inflation. Other changes to the tax code were minor. Capital receipts could be higher than budgeted owing to the EC budget deal struck at the Edinburgh summit meeting in late 1992.

Since October 1992, when the Budget was submitted, the official projection for output growth has been revised down by more than one percentage point to 1¾ per cent. Without further fiscal measures, the government deficit would be higher due to cyclically-induced revenue shortfalls and expenditure increases. The OECD's projections – based on slower growth than in the Budget, but higher inflation – suggest that the general government deficit (on a National Accounts basis) might still be reduced by about 1 percentage point between 1992 and 1993.

On the basis of the OECD projections – which are on a National Accounts basis, but show largely the same profile as the Budget numbers – fiscal tightening in 1993, as measured by the change in the cyclically-adjusted primary budget balance, should be smaller (at close to 1½ per cent of GDP) than in 1992 (about 2 per cent of GDP). The cyclically-adjusted budget balance including interest payments might show an even more impressive cumulative swing towards balance between 1991 and 1993 (amounting to 3 ½ per cent of GDP). However, cyclical developments could slow down the improvement in the budget balance by more than 1 per cent of GDP in both 1992 and 1993 (Table 13). Fiscal restraint and privatisation proceeds have kept the debt to GDP ratio on a downward trend. In 1992 the gross debt to GDP ratio fell to 65 per cent (down from a

Table 13. **Fiscal stance indicators**

Changes in general-government budget balance as a per cent of GDP

	1990	1991	1992	1993	1994
Overall balance	−1.8	−1.1	1.1	0.5	0.4
Primary balance	−1.0	−1.3	1.0	0.4	−0.4
Cyclically-adjusted overall balance	−2.2	−0.6	2.2	1.8	1.4
Cyclically-adjusted primary balance	−1.4	−0.9	2.0	1.6	0.5

Source: OECD estimates.

peak in 1988 of 74 per cent), while the ratio adjusted for Treasury Bills held by the Bank of Portugal fell to 59 per cent.

Monetary and exchange-rate policy

Overview

Monetary policy continued to be geared towards lowering inflation. But despite a switch to fiscal restraint, control of liquidity growth was complicated until mid-1992 by large capital inflows. The authorities' room for manœuvre narrowed with accession of the escudo to the Exchange Rate Mechanism of the EMS with the wide fluctuation band in April 1992 and the subsequent lifting of all remaining capital controls. In the new institutional setting, the authorities stopped specifying a target for liquidity growth in 1993. Keeping the exchange rate stable became the key intermediate target of monetary policy. In November 1992, the central rate of the escudo was adjusted downwards as part of an EMS realignment (Diagram 7).

Structural changes in financial markets

Despite difficulties in liquidity management posed by large capital inflows, the authorities completed the shift to indirect monetary control. Steps were also taken to ease the fragmentation of financial markets. In May 1992, the minimum rate for time deposits from 180 days up to a year was abolished and the rate on demand deposits liberalized, giving credit institutions full freedom to set deposit rates. With the shift away from direct monetary control, the Bank of Portugal

45

Diagram 7. **EXCHANGE-RATE AND INTEREST-RATE DEVELOPMENTS**

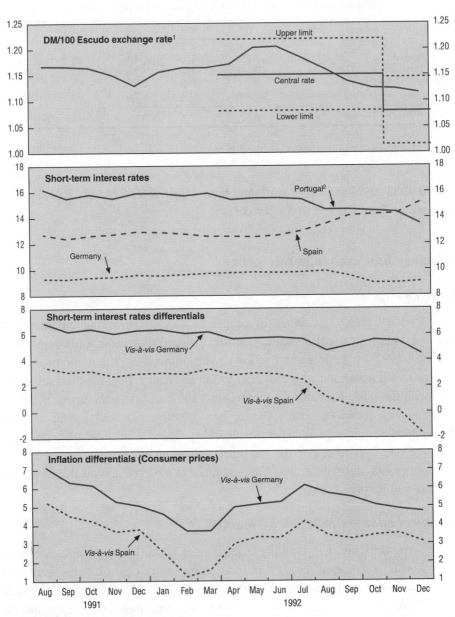

1. Escudo joins wide ERM-band in April 1992.
2. Treasury bills held by the public (over 31 days and up to 90 days).
Source: OECD.

further reduced the spread between its lending rate (the rate of regular provision of liquidity, introduced in April 1991), and the regular draining rate.[9] By August 1992, the difference between the two official rates had shrunk to 2 percentage points as against 5.3 percentage points in April 1991 (Table 14). While the above measures assisted the process of domestic interest-rate convergence, the gap between private lending and deposit rates has remained large, pointing to a persistent weakness of competitive forces in the financial sector.[10]

At the longer end of the market, with a view to achieving budgetary savings, the government placed greater emphasis on auctioning fixed-rate bonds (mostly with a maturity of 5 years) as part of public debt management. Issues of variable

Table 14. **Money-market intervention and lending rates** [1]

	Regular liquidity draining rate (intervention rate)	Rate for regular provision of liquidity (lending rate)	Rate of remuneration of minimum cash reserves
1991			
April	16.5	21.8	
July	16.8	22.0	16.0
	17.0		
August	16.8	21.8	
September	16.0	20.8	
October	15.8	20.3	15.8
November	15.6	20.0	
1992			
February	..	19.5	
March	..	18.9	
April	15.4	17.9	15.4
July	15.3	17.8	14.5
August	15.0	17.0	
	14.0	16.0	
September	Suspension	Suspension	
October	14.0		13.3
November	Suspension		
December	14.0		
1993			
January	13.0		12.8
February	12.8		
March	13.0		
	13.5		

1. Introduced in April 1991.
Source: Bank of Portugal, *Monthly Bulletin.*

indexed bonds ceased in August 1992. More generally, interest rates on all government financial liabilities are now market-determined, reached market levels in 1992, ending the privileged treatment of the public sector as the dominant borrower in financial markets. At the end of 1992, the Treasury's overdraft facility with the central bank was abolished and replaced by a 10-year loan.

The shift to indirect monetary control was followed by the removal of virtually all restrictions on capital flows. Regarding capital **inflows,** the authorities liberalised access to external borrowing by residents as of 1 September 1992. The compulsory, non-remunerated deposit on external borrowing by non-banking resident firms, introduced in July 1990 at a rate of 40 per cent, subsequently lowered in three steps to 25 per cent in July 1992, was abolished the following month. The deposit had aimed at stemming capital inflows. The authorities also terminated restrictions placed on purchases by non-residents of floating-rate bonds (as of 31 October 1992) and fully liberalised all non-resident investments in domestic money-market instruments on 16 December 1992. Regarding capital **outflows,** the last remaining barrier, restrictions on short-term credits extended to non-residents, was dropped on 16 December 1992. Escudo accounts can now be held outside Portugal, while resident banks are allowed to conduct swap transactions with residents and non-residents. The liberalisation of capital movements is likely to enhance competition in financial markets.

Evolution of money and credit

Liquidity growth, measured by L- (liquid assets held by non-financial residents) surged from a low of 13 per cent in March 1991 to nearly 20 per cent in March 1992, driven by a near-tripling of the rate of increase in time deposits and other quasi-monetary liabilities (Diagram 8). Thereafter, the expansion of L- contracted sharply in response to capital outflows and portfolio shifts. Falling to an annualised 12.5 per cent in December 1992, L- growth stayed marginally above the guideline of 12 per cent.

M1- growth followed a different pattern, easing over the twelve months to May 1992, but accelerating sharply thereafter to an annualised rate of 18.7 per cent in January 1993 (Diagram 8). A key factor behind the faster expansion of M1- was the relative decline in time deposit rates, linked to the liberalisation of interest rates on demand deposits in May 1992.[11] As a result, the growth in

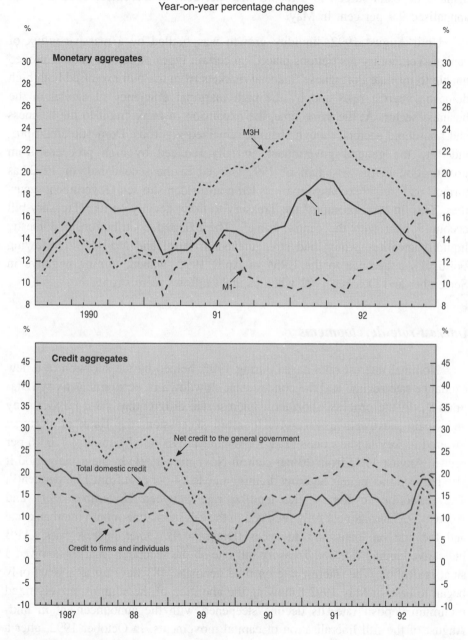

Diagram 8. **MONETARY AND CREDIT AGGREGATES**
Year-on-year percentage changes

Source: Bank of Portugal.

49

demand deposits surged to a record 21.2 per cent in December 1992 from an annualised 9.9 per cent in May.

Until August 1992, liquidity growth was fuelled by a massive influx of capital. Temporary restrictions placed on certain types of capital inflows proved unable to insulate Portuguese financial markets from the pull exercised both high domestic interest rates and by the high marginal efficiency of capital in the business sector. At the same time, the expansion of bank credit to the business and household sectors, though abating, remained vigorous. Domestic credit provided to the general government, initially reduced by high proceeds from privatisation in the first half of 1992, surged in the second half of 1992, as turmoil on foreign exchange markets led non-residents to sell Government securities. This, in turn, prompted the Treasury to draw heavily on its "Treasury-bill account" held with the central bank[12]. The external contribution to domestic liquidity creation, which had strengthened in April and May 1992 following Portugal's adherence to the ERM in April 1992, waned, turning negative in September and October 1992 when capital outflows were strong.

Interest-rate developments

Nominal interest rates eased during 1992, helped by the adoption of a new exchange-rate regime and the concomitant slowdown of economic activity (Diagram 9). In the process, short-term interest rate differentials *vis-à-vis* Germany and Spain narrowed appreciably. In rapid succession, the Bank of Portugal lowered its key lending rate ("rate for regular provision of liquidity") to 16 per cent in August 1992 from 20 per cent in November 1991. In the same period it also reduced the regular liquidity draining rate to 14 per cent from 15.6 per cent[13]. The reduction in the official lending rate between November 1991 and August 1992 was almost fully reflected in the fall in the one-month interbank rate and the rate on loans and advances (Diagram 9). Other interest rates (APB indicative lending rate and Treasury bill rate on the secondary market) showed a smaller decline. The interest rate on time deposits (181 days up to a year) only began to ease in May 1992 following the abolition of the administratively fixed minimum deposit rate. Its decline steepened with the announcement in mid-August of the full liberalisation of capital movements. In October 1992, after a fall in April and September 1992, deposit rates were brought into line with

Diagram 9. **INTEREST RATES**

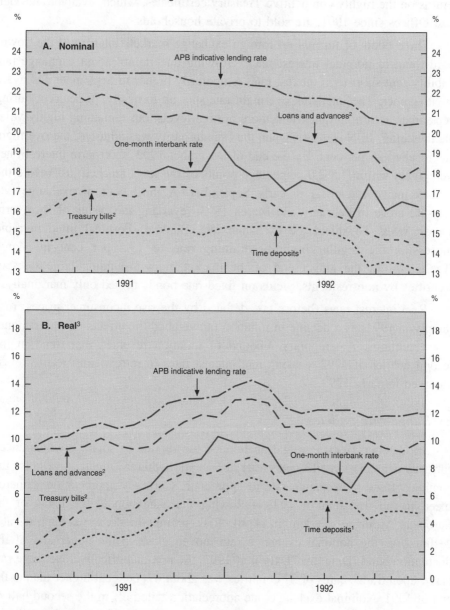

1. 181 days up to one year.
2. 91 days up to 180 days.
3. Adjusted for year-on-year change of the consumer price index.
Sources: Bank of Portugal and OECD.

returns on the highly competitive Treasury certificates, which, available through Post Offices since 1991, are sold to private households.

Three bouts of turmoil on foreign exchange markets interrupted the downward trend of nominal interest rates. Growing uncertainty about exchange rate stability sent short-term interest rates temporarily higher in September and again in November. The interbank overnight rate shot up to nearly 70 per cent during September, returning quickly to more normal levels, but remaining highly volatile thereafter. In November, when the escudo parity was adjusted, the overnight rate reached 25 per cent. By the end of December 1992, short-term interest rates were again within 1.5-2.0 percentage points of the level reached just before the first exchange rate-crisis in early September. A third bout of exchange rate pressure arose in February and March 1993, reversing the easing of short-term interest rates. To shield the exchange rate, Bank of Portugal lifted in rapid succession the regular liquidity draining rate to 13.5 per cent in March (Table 14). At the longer end of the market, notwithstanding large sales of securities by non-residents, yields on fixed-rate bonds firmed only marginally.

Real interest rates (before tax, deflated by the rise inconsumer prices) rose sharply in 1991, as a decline in inflation outweighed the effects of easier monetary conditions. A temporary rebound of inflation reversed that trend in the second quarter of 1992, causing real interest rates to retreat from record levels observed in early 1992.

Exchange-rate policies

In October 1990, Portugal abandoned the regime of small, pre-announced currency depreciations, 13 years after its inception, thereby creating room for the nominal effective exchange rate to appreciate. Currency appreciation gathered speed in the first half of 1992, following the accession to the ERM of the European Monetary System in April. Risk premia in domestic interest rates declined, as the nominal exchange rate moved close to the upper end of the fluctuation band (Diagram 7). By mid-1992, the nominal effective exchange rate based upon trade shares of 27 countries was about 6¼ per cent higher than at the end of 1991. Nominal exchange rate appreciation tailed off in the second half of 1992, curbed by sudden exchange rate changes in Europe. This, together with the fall in the inflation differential (as measured by changes in consumer prices) held the year-on-year rise in the real effective exchange rate to 9.2 per cent in 1992.

Using changes in relative prices of manufactured exports suggests a much smaller rise in the relative price of tradeable goods (2.2 per cent in 1992), confirming a trend manifest since 1986 when Portugal joined the EC. While relative unit labour costs in manufacturing and relative consumer prices surged by about 30 per cent between 1986 and 1992, relative unit values of manufactured exports hardly changed. The divergence between cost and price developments may not have represented an intolerable profit squeeze, given the initially high rate of return on capital in the exposed sector.

See-sawing since mid-1992, the nominal effective exchange rate weakened in August, but recovered in October following the first 1992 EMS realignment in September. While Portugal maintained its bilateral rates with ERM-countries, Spain and Italy devalued the central value of their currency in the ERM. The subsequent withdrawal of the lira and the pound sterling from the ERM accentuated the recovery of the nominal effective exchange rate. In November 1992, a third EMS realignment reduced the central value of the escudo and the peseta by 6 per cent. The parity adjustment left the nominal effective exchange rate of the escudo broadly unchanged (Diagram 10).

Structural policies

Since accession to the EC, substantial progress has been accomplished in reforming the environment in which goods, financial and labour markets operate[14]. While the pace of structural adjustment and institutional reform was very rapid between 1986 – when Portugal joined the EC – and 1989, it has slowed somewhat in recent years. However, privatisation of the large state-owned enterprise sector has been proceeding rapidly since 1989, and financial markets have been liberalised (see above).

The Portuguese **labour market** has been characterised by a considerable degree of wage flexibility, coupled with employment rigidity (see below). So far, the benefits from wage flexibility appear to have outweighed the drawbacks from employment rigidity and labour-market legislation has eased some restrictions on lay-offs since 1989. On the other hand, unemployment benefit coverage and generosity were improved and the use of short-term contracts restricted (1989 and 1991). In 1991, legislative changes included the progressive reduction in the working week from 44 to 40 hours by 1995 and the possibility of dismissal for

Diagram 10. **EXCHANGE RATE OF THE ESCUDO**
VIS-A-VIS SELECTED CURRENCIES[1]

Index 1986 = 100

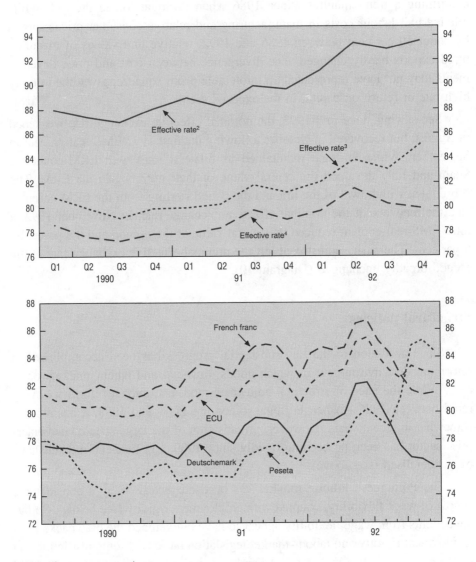

1. Units of currency per escudo.
2. Based upon trade shares of 27 countries.
3. Based upon the trade shares of Germany, France, United Kingdom, Italy and Spain.
4. Based upon the trade shares of Germany, France and Spain.

Source: OECD estimates.

failure to meet job requirements. In July 1992, strike regulations were modified by widening the scope of the compulsory "minimum service" regulation to the transportation, energy, mining public health sectors. Human capital formation was enhanced by rapid increases in training expenditures largely owing to EC transfers. In the four years to 1992, the volume of spending on education and training was scheduled to increase annually at $7\frac{1}{2}$ and 10 per cent, respectively, with the accent on training of school-leavers.

Market discipline has been fostered by the integration of markets in the context of the Single Market. In addition, the government has liberalised markets on a broad front. Apart from the liberalisation of financial markets and privatisation, which are described elsewhere, private enterprises are now allowed to operate in air transport, telecommunications and broadcasting. Furthermore, price liberalisation has proceeded, and many, mainly industrial, goods have been excluded from administrative price control. Rent controls, however, still exist for apartments rented under old contracts. A review of **competition policy** aims at eliminating sectoral exemptions for pursuing enterprises for restrictive business practices. In addition, a reformulation of the merger control regime was submitted to the Government for approval at the end of 1992.

Since 1989, consumer protection has been tightened in line with EC recommendations, and the public display of prices has been made mandatory. At the same time, the set-up of large retail outlets was regulated, which might entail costs to consumers in terms of restricted choice and higher prices. Inflation in the sheltered sector remains high, suggesting that competitive pressure is still rather weak.

Environmental quality is largely intact in Portugal, although there are local problems of water quality and air pollution. As strong growth is intensifying pressures on the environment, the authorities have started to put more emphasis on stringent environmental regulations and monitoring. The implementation of the Framework Law on the Environment, which focuses on improving water quality, is practically complete. Implementation is being achieved by programme contracts. Pulp companies, for instance, invested Esc 17 billion in pollution abatement equipment. An environmental financial package subsidising investment in pollution control equipment by up to 50 per cent of outlays is under consideration. Negotiations with municipalities and industry are currently underway aimed at a reduction in water pollution by 50 per cent by the year 2000. This would bring emissions into line with European average levels. Investment outlays for this purpose are large, totalling an estimated Esc 300 billion for new infrastructure and Esc 125 billion for upgrading existing treatment facilities. Apart from tighter regulation of water pollution, new legislation concerning air pollution, environmental impact assessments, waste and nature conservation has been passed.

IV. Recent trends and projections

After a period of very satisfactory output and employment performance in the years immediately following Portugal's accession to the EC (1986-90), activity weakened in 1991 and 1992 due to a marked deterioration in net exports, while domestic demand growth remained brisk (Diagram 11). Nevertheless, output growth remained slightly above the OECD average and the rate of unemployment was one of the lowest among Member countries. With a significant tightening of fiscal policy, however, Portugal seems to be entering a phase of slower expansion, but progress on the inflation front achieved since mid-1991 should become more pronounced in 1993-94.

Recent trends

Persistently-strong domestic demand

Contrary to expectations, real total domestic demand remained buoyant in 1991, rising by 4 per cent again in 1992, a rate 2½ points above the OECD average (Table 15). The composition of domestic demand, however, changed somewhat between 1991 and 1992, with the slowdown in both private and public consumption being offset by renewed strength in investment growth.

With little employment growth, a slowdown in real wage gains and an adjustment in pensions less than the rate of inflation, real household disposable income growth eased further in 1992, to 2¾ per cent, back to a rate similar to the average in the second half of the 1980s. At the same time, the saving ratio continued to decline, to 21½ per cent of disposable income, due in part to the deceleration of inflation and its positive impact on households' net worth.[15]

Diagram 11. **EVOLUTION OF ECONOMIC PERFORMANCE**

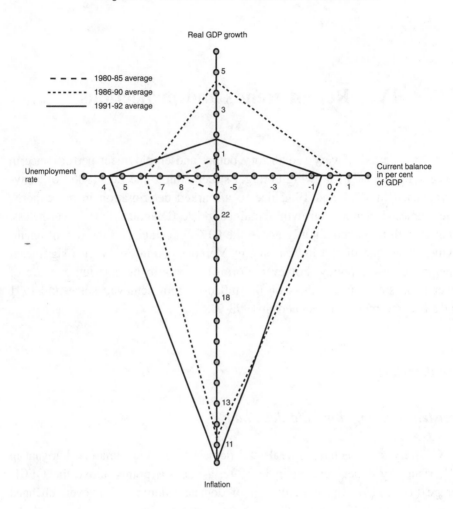

Real GDP growth

- - - - 1980-85 average
······· 1986-90 average
——— 1991-92 average

Unemployment rate

Current balance in per cent of GDP

Inflation

Note: The diagram plots major macro-economic performance indicators along the four rays from the origin. Measuring scales are chosen such that performance improves with distance from the origin except in the case of the current balance where data are presented solely for information.
Source: OECD.

Overall, the growth of real private consumption slowed to 4 per cent in 1992. While non-durable consumers' expenditure eased substantially, sales of passenger cars have been rising at an annual rate of over 20 per cent.

Table 15. **Recent macroeconomic developments**

Percentage changes, volume, 1985 prices

	1987 Current prices Esc. billion	1988	1989	1990	1991	1992[1]
A. Demand and output						
Private consumption	3 335.7	6.6	3.3	5.3	5.2	4.0
Government consumption	787.8	5.3	2.8	1.5	3.0	1.8
Gross fixed capital formation	1 250.8	15.0	5.6	5.9	2.5	4.9
Final domestic demand	5 374.3	8.3	3.8	4.9	4.3	4.0
Change in stockbuilding[2]	171.0	−0.8	0.6	0.7	0	0.2
Total domestic demand	5 545.3	7.4	4.3	5.4	4.1	4.1
Exports of goods and services	1 774.7	10.2	13.3	9.5	1.1	6.7
Imports of goods and services	2 145.2	16.1	9.1	10.1	4.9	9.8
Change in foreign balance[2]	−370.6	−4.5	0.2	−1.9	−2.6	−3.3
GDP at market prices	5 174.7	3.9	5.2	4.4	2.2	1.4
B. Household's appropriation account						
Compensation of employees	2 386.6	14.6	15.4	21.0	19.2	15.0
Income from property and others	1 805.6	14.0	22.3	18.1	16.0	13.5
Current transfers received	1 167.4	12.7	14.8	16.8	15.5	12.5
Total income	5 359.6	14.0	17.5	19.1	17.3	14.0
less: Direct taxes	218.1	48.6	44.7	9.2	31.2	21.7
Current transfers paid	658.4	14.0	16.3	19.1	16.9	18.1
Disposable income	4 483.1	12.2	16.0	19.9	16.4	12.6
Consumers' expenditure	3 335.7	17.2	15.8	18.7	17.9	13.6
Saving ratio	25.6	22.3	22.4	23.3	22.3	21.6
Real disposable income	3 580.5	2.0	3.5	6.5	3.9	2.8

1. OECD estimates.
2. As a percent of GDP in the previous period.
Sources: National Institute of Statistics and OECD, *National Accounts* and estimates.

Gross fixed capital formation rebounded in 1992 from its depressed levels following the Gulf crisis. The rebound in gross capital formation was reinforced by renewed strength in foreign direct investment inflows, notably in the tourism and insurance sectors, and the availability of ample EC funds, which supported investment in construction. Domestic financing conditions have been less favourable. Profitability has fallen back since the second half of the 1980s, as changes in the exchange-rate policy intensified foreign competitive pressures. Although the squeeze in business profitability was probably weaker in 1992, appreciation-induced price restraint, as in the previous two years, remained strong in the tradeables sector (see below).

According to business surveys, the high cost of borrowing combined with weaker demand prospects have weighed on capital formation. Indeed, domestic borrowing rates, though declining slowly, are still at some 18 to 20 per cent. The compulsory non-remunerated 40 per cent deposit at the Central Bank of all capital raised abroad by non-financial enterprises (introduced in February 1991 and removed at the end of August 1992) added to the borrowing costs of large enterprises. Furthermore, equity capital is costly, given the depressed state of the stock market, which has fallen by about two-thirds since early 1989.

Tighter control of government expenditure led to some moderation in job creation in the public sector, and real public consumption growth has slowed from 3 per cent in 1991 to 1½ per cent in 1992. Stockbuilding increased substantially, partly in response to a shift in exchange-rate expectations. Reflecting cyclical differences in domestic demand and a return to high import elasticities, the negative contribution of the real foreign balance to output growth widened markedly in 1992 despite an improvement in export performance. Thus, GDP growth weakened further from 2¼ per cent in 1991 to 1½ per cent in 1992.

Reflecting developments in most sub-sectors in manufacturing, industrial production has been falling since the second quarter of 1991, at an estimated rate of 2¼ per cent on average in 1992. As in 1991, real value added in agriculture, forestry and fisheries also dropped markedly (by more than 11 per cent), a consequence of the severe drought. Activity in construction remained strong. The above-average growth in both financial and non-financial services recorded in 1990 and 1991 continued into 1992 (around 3 and 5 per cent, respectively).

The labour market

Emerging signs of easing labour-market conditions

Extremely tight labour-market conditions in 1991 and early 1992 seem to have eased later in the year[16] (Table 16). Employment rose little in 1992 compared with 3 per cent in 1991. The growth in both self-employment and dependent employment slowed down markedly, with the number of workers in industry contracting during 1992. Productivity per employee rebounded to 1¼ per cent in

Table 16. **Labour market indicators**

Percentages

	1987	1988	1989	1990	1991	1992[1]
Participation rate[2]	71.2	71.4	71.9	72.4	74.0	70.7
Male	84.9	84.5	84.9	84.9	85.5	81.4
Female	58.4	59.2	59.7	60.7	63.2	60.9
Civilian labour force (growth rates)	1.0	1.1	1.5	1.8	2.2	..
Male	–0.3	0.2	1.4	0.9	0.7	..
Female	2.8	2.5	1.6	2.9	4.0	..
Employment (growth rates)	2.6	2.6	2.2	2.3	3.0	..
Male	1.1	1.5	2.0	1.4	1.4	..
Female	4.9	4.1	2.5	3.5	5.0	..
Dependent employment	2.2	4.4	3.5	2.9	1.4	..
Full-time	2.3	2.4	2.3	1.8	2.6	..
Part-time	7.4	5.4	0.7	9.0	8.4	..
Agriculture	3.9	–4.4	–6.3	–4.1	0.5	..
Industry	4.9	3.3	2.9	0.9	0.3	..
Services	0.2	5.5	5.8	5.9	6.0	..
Unemployment rate[3]	7.1	5.8	5.0	4.7	4.1	4.2
Male	5.3	4.1	3.4	3.2	2.8	..
Female	9.5	8.0	7.2	6.6	5.8	..
Youth (15-24)	16.2	13.1	11.4	10.0	9.1	..
Long-term unemployment[4]	47.3	42.0	38.2	33.9	30.2	22.7[5]
Job vacancies[3]	0.16	0.21	0.22	0.17	0.17	0.16

1. Break in series due to changes in the Quarterly Labour Force Survey; participation rates are the averages of the first three quarters.
2. Per cent of working-age population.
3. Per cent of the labour force.
4. Per cent of total unemployment.
5. Average of the first two quarters.
Sources: National Institute of Statistics and OECD *Labour Force Statistics.*

1992, after falling by ³/₄ per cent in 1991. However, sharp rises in part-time employment since 1989[17] have led to a decline in the average work week, and increases in hourly productivity were much stronger.[18] Whatever the measure chosen, however, the period of above-EC average growth in labour productivity in Portugal since 1985 came to an end in 1991-92.

With less favourable labour-market conditions, participation have probably increased less than in the previous few years, reducing labour force growth after two years of steady gains (by 2 per cent on average) and damping the rise in unemployment (Table 16). The rate of unemployment, which remained at 4 per cent of the labour force in the first half of 1992, started rising thereafter. Taking the changes in the definitions of the quarterly labour-force survey into account,[19] the unemployment rate is estimated to have reached 4¼ per cent on average in 1992, compared with 4.1 per cent a year earlier.[20] Long-term unemployment was further reduced to 23 per cent of total unemployment in 1992, down from nearly one half in 1987. Youth unemployment seems to have remained largely unchanged in 1992, but the removal of those aged 13 and 14 from the labour force statistics makes any comparison hazardous.

The labour market in perspective

In the present phase of adjustment, one of Portugal's great assets lies in the flexibility of the labour market.[21] Up to the mid-1980s, when the rate of unemployment reached a peak of 8¾ per cent, unemployment developments followed those in other countries. Shocks in the previous two decades (the Colonial Wars, the 1974 Revolution and the return of emigrants from Africa) were absorbed without lasting problems. Since the mid-1980s, the Portuguese labour market performance has compared very favourably with the other OECD countries. Job creation was rapid and unemployment fell to close to 4 per cent in 1992.

Over the whole period since 1960, employment has risen on average by ¾ per cent a year, while real GDP has increased by 4¾ per cent a year. This compares with rates in the OECD area of 1 and 3½ per cent, respectively. Until 1974, employment remained flat while GDP grew at an average annual rate of 6½ per cent. In 1974-86, output growth slowed to 2¾ per cent *per annum* while employment expanded at a rate of ¾ per cent on average. The pace of job creation picked up with EC accession in 1986 (2¼ per cent on average in 1986-92) as real GDP growth accelerated to an annual average of 3¾ per cent (Diagram 12).

While overall employment increased somewhat less than in the OECD area, sectoral employment shifts were large: the steep decline in farm employment since 1960 (from 40 per cent of the total to a still high 12 per cent in 1991[22]) has been more than compensated by increases in manufacturing and services, includ-

Diagram 12. **THE LABOUR MARKET**

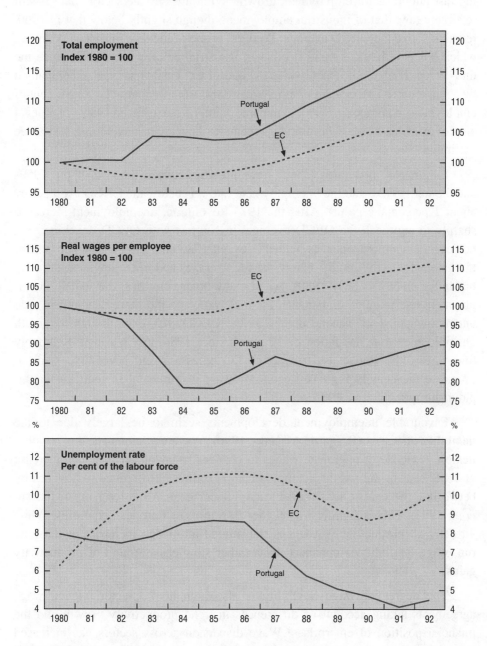

Source: OECD.

ing fast public sector employment growth. While the service sector share is still relatively low, that of industrial employment, though slightly below that in 1960, remains above the OECD average. Portugal is one of the few European countries which has not shown a trend decline in industrial employment levels since the mid-1970s. High employment since the end of the 1980s has been accompanied by a marked rise in the share of employees on short-term contracts (22 per cent of employment contracts in 1991, compared with 13 per cent in 1980-82). Illegal employment, notably of immigrants, seems to have been developing fast since the mid-1980s.

Emigration moderated labour force growth between the end of the 1950s and the mid-1970s, and the unemployment rate was below the OECD average (by about 1 percentage point). After the 1974 Revolution, unemployment increased sharply to approach the OECD average. In contrast with OECD developments, however, unemployment was halved between 1986 and 1992 to 4¼ per cent of the labour force (5¼ points below the EC average) and unemployment duration has fallen since the early 1980s. As in many other countries, the female unemployment rate is much higher than the male rate, and the share of youth in total unemployment is the second highest in the OECD area, even though the youth unemployment rate has fallen by 10 points since 1984, to 9 per cent. Relatively low wages, the impact on growth of EC accession and successive steps to liberalise the heavily regulated economy were instrumental in reducing unemployment quickly after 1986.

Favourable unemployment developments seem to be largely due to the flexibility of wages (Braga de Macedo, 1990). Wage equations attest to a rather flexible response of aggregate wages to changes in unemployment. An increase of 1 per cent in the rate of unemployment is estimated to reduce real wages by between 1 per cent (OECD, 1992) and 1.4 per cent in the long run (Modesto *et al.* 1992). This is significantly higher than in most European countries. While virtually all productivity growth is transmitted into wage increases in the long run, wage flexibility is enhanced by a rather slow pass-through of productivity gains.

The degree of wage flexibility is also high at the sectoral level, wage agreements taking account of differences in trend productivity growth and the financial position of enterprises. Wage dispersion across sectors has increased over the last decade and is much greater than in the other European countries.

Employment levels in low wage industries had, therefore, not fallen until 1990, contrary to developments in most other European countries.

In the 1980s, several tripartite social agreements have yielded non-binding guidelines for aggregate wage increases. Since 1986 they have become based on prospective, rather than past, inflation, which permitted the government to influence price expectations. How effective wage agreements have been in improving the trade-off between unemployment and inflation is unclear. They definitely had an impact in the years when agreements were struck. However, stubbornly-high inflation usually led to a catch-up of wages in the years when there was no agreement. Finally, the revision of pay scales and the upgrading of certain jobs in the public sector since 1989, which increased public sector wages significantly, may also have influenced private sector wage claims.

Some structural and institutional features may have influenced labour market developments. Meagre unemployment compensation – benefits per unemployed amounted to 27 per cent of compensation per employee in 1991 – may have been a disincentive for workers to become and stay unemployed. The relatively small rate of cover (41 per cent of registered unemployed[23] in 1991, up from 24 per cent in 1985) and strict entitlement criteria (540 days of contribution) outweighed the comparatively generous replacement ratio (65 per cent of previous average wage within a ceiling over a 10-30 month period), very similar to those in France and Germany but lower than in Spain. However, nearly 40 per cent of all recipients of unemployment compensation receive social assistance at a lower rate, *i.e.* 70 to 100 per cent of the minimum wage depending upon the family size. First-time job-seekers have been entitled to compensation since 1988, subject to a number of conditions.

The minimum wage, which was instituted after the 1974 Revolution, does not seem to have had much influence on the wage formation process in recent years. Its real value declined sharply until 1985, with some catch-up thereafter. In 1991, the minimum wage in nominal terms amounted to 45 per cent of the average wage in the non-farm sector, compared with a peak of 56 per cent in 1985. Only 6½ per cent of employees, however, are currently paid at the minimum wage level, and minimum wage levels for young people (below 18) are 25 per cent below those for adults. Non-wage labour costs are lower than in most OECD countries, with employers' social-security contributions amounting to some 24.5 per cent of gross wages.

Some progress in lowering inflation

With still tight labour-market conditions and continuing strong domestic demand growth, domestic cost pressures did not ease and the real wage rate in the private sector increased more than labour productivity, though to a much lesser extent than in 1991. Despite the wage agreement reached by the social partners of an annual increase of 9¾ per cent in 1992, private compensation per employee rose by 13 per cent (Table 17). While pay rises were far above average in metallurgy, and some private services, wage moderation was noticeable in some traditional industries, such as textiles. Reflecting the tailing-off of the public-sector pay-scale reform, government wage increases declined markedly, but nevertheless remained higher than in the private sector. The pick-up in private sector productivity, together with weaker wage gains, triggered a sizeable deceleration in unit labour costs in 1992. More importantly than domestic costs, falling import prices have contributed markedly to reducing cost inflation in 1992. According to calculations by the Bank of Portugal (Bank of Portugal, 1992), "unit costs of imports", which had risen by 12 per cent in 1990, slowed down to

Table 17. **Wage and price formation**

Per cent rate of growth

	1988	1989	1990	1991	1992[1]
Compensation per employee					
Total	9.7	11.4	17.8	17.6	14.7
Private	7.2	10.4	16.3	16.2	12.9
Contractual wages	9.0	10.7	13.8	14.1	11
Unit labour costs	10.2	9.7	16.0	16.7	13.4
Private consumption deflator	10.0	12.1	12.6	12.0	9.5
Projected inflation[2]	6	6	10	10¾	9¼
Import prices	11.5	8.7	6.4	1.2	−3.5
Export prices	8.8	10.9	6.0	0.9	−1.5
GDP deflator	11.6	13.0	14.3	13.6	12.8
Memorandum item:					
Labour productivity	1.3	2.9	2.1	−0.7	1.1

1. OECD estimates.
2. Budget projections for consumer prices excluding rent.
Source: OECD, *National Accounts.*

an estimated rate of 1.6 per cent in 1992, largely due to the effective appreciation of the exchange rate and falling international inflation.[24]

The easing in consumer price inflation, which started in the summer of 1991, continued into early 1992 (Diagram 13). But adjustments in the coverage and rates of the VAT (see above) and a major rise in tobacco prices pushed inflation to year-on-year rates of 9.5 per cent in April-July, subsiding thereafter to 7.4 per cent in March 1993. Overall, consumer prices rose by 8.9 per cent in 1992, compared with 11.4 per cent in 1991. The Government's inflation rate objective of 7 to 9 per cent in 1992, embodied in the 1992 Budget, was thus met. Excluding the impact of changes in VAT would have improved the performance of inflation by an estimated 1½ to 2 percentage points. However, underlying inflation (excluding food and energy) remained high, at an average rate of 11.8 per cent in 1992. Since the last peak in October 1990, the year-on-year rises in the prices of non-tradeables were halved to 10¾ per cent at the end of 1992, while tradeables inflation fell by 2 points to 7 per cent. The consumer-price differential with the EC average (including rent) fell back from 7 percentage points in 1991 to 5¾ points in 1992.

Foreign trade and the current balance

Both export and import growth accelerated in 1992 (Table 18). A stronger relative cyclical position, with real total domestic demand growing about 2½ points above that of Portugal's major trading partners boosted merchandise-import growth to a rate of 9¾ per cent. With merchandise-import prices falling by 5½ per cent, the higher apparent income elasticity reflects, in part, the deterioration in the relative competitiveness of domestic products. Due to the pick-up in investment, imports of equipment goods, notably transport equipment, rose sharply, while growth in imports of consumer goods, other than food, remained substantial.

Exports were remarkably resilient in the face of weak OECD activity in 1992, following weakness in 1991 linked to the Gulf war.[25] Merchandise exports picked up from a ¾ per cent rate in real terms in 1991 to an estimated 6½ per cent in 1992. With export markets for Portuguese goods growing by 3¾ per cent in 1992, as in 1991, earlier losses of market shares have been regained. Exports of energy products and transport material were strongest, as they rallied from their depressed levels in 1991. In the first nine months of 1992, market penetration of

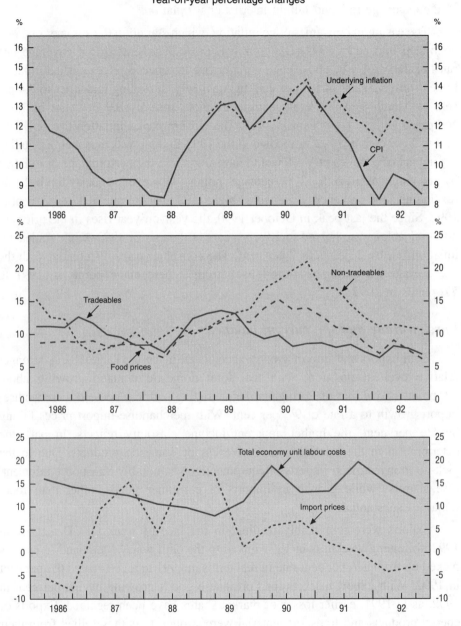

Diagram 13. **INFLATION DEVELOPMENTS**

Year-on-year percentage changes

Sources: Bank of Portugal and OECD.

Table 18. **Balance of payments**

Billion escudos

	1990	1991	1992[1]
Exports (Fob)	2 320	2 339	2 477
Imports (Fob)	3 287	3 473	3 672
Trade balance	–967	–1 134	–1 195
Services, net	194	160	120
of which: Tourism	380	391	341
Investment income, net	–34	11	70
Transfers, net	782	868	952
Private	638	666	643
Public	144	202	412
Current balance	–26	–96	–6
(as per cent of GDP)	(–0.3)	(–1.0)	(–0.1)
Medium and long-term capital, net	511	587	–82
of which: Foreign direct investment, net	321	331	254
Basic balance	485	491	–88
Short-term capital and unrecorded transactions, net	80	263	195
Balance on non-monetary transactions	565	754	107
(as per cent of GDP)	(6.6)	(7.6)	(0.9)
Short-term capital of private monetary institutions, net	–47	113	–70
Balance on official settlements	518	868	13

1. Provisional figures.
Source: Bank of Portugal.

Portuguese goods strengthened in Germany, France and the United Kingdom, but fell in the United States and Spain.

The return to market-share gains in 1992 can be explained in part by a fall in relative export prices (Diagram 14). Faced with the rise in the nominal effective exchange-rate between October 1990, when the crawling-peg regime of the escudo was terminated, and mid-1992, which involved an even larger real appreciation of the escudo in terms of relative unit labour costs, exporters have compressed their profit margins. According to the Bank of Portugal, the actual fall in export margins was probably less marked than suggested by the difference in price and labour cost growth, as prices of imported inputs fell.[26] Moreover,

Diagram 14. INDICATORS OF COMPETITIVENESS AND FOREIGN TRADE

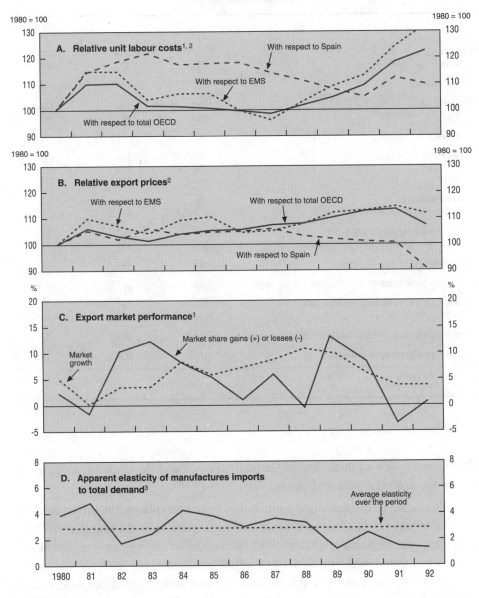

1980 = 100

A. Relative unit labour costs[1, 2]

With respect to Spain

With respect to EMS

With respect to total OECD

1980 = 100

B. Relative export prices[2]

With respect to EMS

With respect to total OECD

With respect to Spain

%

C. Export market performance[1]

Market share gains (+) or losses (-)

Market growth

%

D. Apparent elasticity of manufactures imports to total demand[3]

Average elasticity over the period

1. Manufacturing.
2. In a common currency.
3. Domestic demand plus exports, in volume.
Source: OECD estimates.

70

costs are still probably lower relative to productivity levels than in most OECD countries, especially for new plants.

Fluctuations in price or cost competitiveness have not been the only determinant of trade trends. Important structural changes have been taking place in Portugal in the wake of EC accession. Despite a deterioration in the relative competitive position, market-share gains have been sustained, reflecting in particular an improvement in supply-side factors largely due to the large inflows of foreign direct investment. Reflecting the significant deterioration in the relative price competitiveness of domestic products,[27] but also increasing integration in the EC, import penetration has risen markedly since about mid-1989.

The current account is estimated to have returned to approximate balance in 1992, after a deficit of 1 per cent of GDP in 1991, as a marked deterioration in the trade balance was more than offset by a surge in official transfers from the EC, which had been delayed in 1991. With a further shrinking in the surplus on tourism,[28] linked to the general slowdown in activity and the weakness of the US dollar, the surplus on services declined in 1992. The surplus on private transfers also diminished in line with falling migrants' remittances. The surplus on net investment income widened sharply in 1992, reflecting higher interest payments on net foreign reserves which amounted to 8.7 per cent of GDP in 1992.

Capital movements

The balance on medium-term and long-term capital moved into deficit in 1992, as turmoil in the EMS in the second half of the year triggered heavy sales of domestic securities by non-residents (Table 18). In addition, foreign direct investment and purchases of real estate contracted from 3½ per cent to 2½ per cent of GDP. Overall, the balance on medium- and long-term capital was in deficit to the tune of nearly 1 per cent of GDP in 1992, contrasting with a 5 per cent surplus a year earlier. As a result, the basic balance shifted into deficit after recording a sizeable surplus in 1992. However, narrowly defined (current account balance plus foreign direct investment), the basic balance continued to show a surplus to the tune of 2½ per cent of GDP. The surplus on short-term capital also remained comfortable, largely due to the item "short-term operations, errors and omissions", which may suggest that the capital controls introduced since 1990

71

and removed in mid-1992, have probably been partly circumvented. Overall, net official reserves, after surging in 1991, rose only marginally in 1992.

The outlook to end-1994

The OECD's short-term projections are based on the usual technical assumption that economic policies remain unchanged until the end of 1994. In line with the 1993 Budget and the 1992-95 convergence programme "Q2", the general-government budget deficit might narrow to 4¼ per cent in 1994, largely due to decreasing interest rates and cuts in state expenditure, but also to some extent to fiscal drag. Monetary conditions might ease, with short-term and long-term interest rates coming down in both nominal and real terms. The present OECD projections put annual export market growth for Portugal's manufactures at 2¾ per cent in 1993 and 4¾ per cent in 1994. These figures are moderately lower than those published in *Economic Outlook 52*, December 1992. Two other assumptions that underlie the present projections are an oil price of $ 17 a barrel in the first half of 1993, with no change in real terms thereafter, and fixed nominal exchange rates.

As a result of sustained fiscal consolidation and wage moderation, some unwinding of macroeconomic imbalances should take place, though activity is likely to remain relatively weak (Table 19). Domestic demand should cool on account of reduced growth in private consumption and gross fixed capital formation, while the strongly negative contribution of net exports to output growth might shrink by ¾ percentage points. Overall, real GDP growth might slow in 1993 to a rate of nearly 1 per cent, picking up to 1¾ in 1994, below the growth rate of potential output, but close to the EC average.

Wages in the private sector are not yet settled for 1993. On the basis of current negotiations, some wage moderation is incorporated in the projections, which, coupled with tight fiscal policies, will restrain the growth of households' real disposable income. However, declining inflation should reduce the propensity to save, thereby sustaining private consumption. In line with the ceilings on primary budget expenditure, little growth in real public consumption would mark a break with past trends. Business surveys and a further squeeze on profit margins suggest that investment growth, notably in construction, should slow down markedly in 1993. Renewed investment strength in 1994 would be under-

Table 19. **The short-term outlook**
Percentage changes

	1992	1993	1994
Demand and output (1985 prices)			
Private consumption	4.0	3.3	3.0
Government consumption	1.8	1.5	1.0
Gross fixed investment	4.9	2.8	4.2
Final domestic demand	4.0	3.0	3.1
Change in stockbuilding [1]	0.2	0	0
Total domestic demand	4.1	2.9	3.0
Exports of goods and services	6.7	3.6	6.6
Imports of goods and services	9.8	6.1	7.2
Charge in foreign balance [1]	–3.3	–2.6	–2.1
GDP	1.4	0.9	1.7
Inflation			
Private consumption deflator	9.5	7.5	6.0
GDP deflator	12.8	8.5	6.3
Labour market			
Employment	0.3	–0.2	–0.3
Unemployment rate	4.5	5.1	5.7
Trade balance [2]	–10	–12	–11½
Current balance [2]	–0	–½	–¾
Saving ratio [3]	21.6	20.4	19.2

1. Change as a per cent of GDP in the previous period.
2. As a per cent of GDP.
3. As a per cent of households' disposable income.
Source: OECD estimates and projections.

pinned by EC structural funds, stronger export growth and some rebuilding of profits.

On the basis of unchanged nominal exchange rates, the escudo would experience a slight real appreciation, leading to further losses in cost competitiveness in 1993. However, as in the period 1989-92, exporters are likely to largely absorb the currency appreciation through further cuts in their profit margins. Export growth should abate in 1993 owing to weaker market growth, but pick up in 1994 with improving price competitiveness and strengthening foreign demand. Overall, Portugal will probably record some market-share gains over the period. In line with increases in final sales and an average demand elasticity of imports, import growth should weaken this year, picking up in 1994 to a rate of 6½ per cent.

Employment is expected to adjust with a lag to the slowdown of output growth, falling slightly in 1993 and 1994. The unemployment rate may keep rising to 5¾ per cent of the labour force in 1994. With easing labour markets, real wage gains will be smaller, possibly falling below productivity gains in both 1993 and 1994. The rise in unit labour costs could be halved by 1994, and consumer price inflation should continue to subside to a rate of 6 per cent by 1994, the differential with the EC average falling from 5¾ percentage points in 1992 to 2¾ points in 1994. With worsening terms of trade, the current deficit is likely to widen progressively to 1½ per cent of GDP in 1994.

The main risks in this projection attach to cost and price developments, and to the speed of the slowdown in domestic demand. Domestic demand remained stronger than projected in both 1991 and 1992, fuelled by higher real wage gains and sharper falls in the saving ratio. Should the labour market remain tight, wage moderation would not occur to the projected extent and domestic demand could remain buoyant. Disinflation might proceed at a slower pace, thus jeopardising competitiveness and leading to a stronger deterioration in the current balance. Macroeconomic imbalances would persist and the process of nominal convergence could be delayed.

V. Conclusions

The Portuguese economy grew rapidly up to 1991 and convergence towards EC real income levels was proceeding. Export growth benefited from integration in the EC markets and from large foreign direct investment, while investment increased its share in GDP considerably. The supply of capital and labour, however, did not match the surge in demand, and the consequent overheating of the economy found its most visible expression in renewed inflationary pressure between 1989 and 1990, when consumer price inflation peaked at a rate of 14½ per cent. The Government therefore adopted a convergence programme in November 1991, calling for a sharp fall in inflation and further cuts in the government deficit. The tightening of policy, including fiscal consolidation, and the OECD-wide slowdown contributed to reducing output growth to 1½ per cent in 1992. Domestic demand proved to be very resilient, at least until mid-1992 and is estimated to have risen by close to 4 per cent in 1992 on average. Activity was dampened, however, by a widening in the negative contribution of external trade to GDP growth. Nevertheless, the current account moved towards balance, reflecting a further improvement in the terms of trade and a larger surplus in investment income and EC transfers. The cooling down of the overheated economy translated into some slack in goods and labour markets, showing up during 1992 in a gentle rise in unemployment from very low levels. Along with falling import prices, this helped curb price and wage inflation. Despite a marked increase in VAT, consumer-price inflation dipped to just below 9 per cent, the upper end of the official target range. In the sheltered sector, however, inflation is still hovering in the double-digit range. Given an inflation differential of 5 per cent with the average of the EMS countries, nominal convergence is still distant, calling for strong, persistent efforts to reduce inflation.

According to the Secretariat's projections, economic growth might slow further to about 1 per cent in 1993, before picking up somewhat in 1994 as lower interest rates in Europe begin to promote recovery and the external outlook improves. Slower growth in disposable income together with fiscal consolidation should dampen the growth in both private and public consumption, while net trade could be less of a drag on output growth. Strengthening foreign demand and lower interest rates might lead to some pick-up in exports and investment in 1994. However, the unemployment rate might increase towards 6 per cent by the end of 1994. Dampened by a further widening of economic slack in goods and labour markets, consumer price inflation may ease to 6 per cent in 1994, the lowest rise in 20 years. The projections accordingly indicate considerable progress in terms of nominal convergence with EC partners; nevertheless, more will need to be done, as inflation will still remain significantly above the Maastricht target.

Important risks attach to this scenario. In order to reduce inflation as projected, the rise in unit labour costs, which was $13\frac{1}{2}$ per cent in 1992, needs to fall rapidly. While wage flexibility has been high in the past, wage inflation could fall less fast than projected as the labour market is still close to full employment. A continuation of high wage inflation could pose serious problems for traditional export sectors as profit margins have already been squeezed significantly in recent years. Should wage inflation be more stubborn and policies remain geared to current objectives, the deceleration in output growth could be stronger than projected. If, on the other hand, policies were eased in response to such a development, nominal convergence would be delayed and policy credibility impaired. This could make disinflation even more costly in the future.

The present convergence programme ("Q2") calls for tight monetary policies, aimed at a stable exchange rate, and these are seen as reducing the inflation differential against the best-performing EC member countries quickly. Fiscal policy should help in achieving the inflation target by reducing the budget deficit to a maximum of 3 per cent of GDP by 1995. The Government intends that the reduction of the deficit should be achieved by expenditure control, the Government setting multi-annual targets for primary expenditure in nominal terms. The fall in the deficit should dampen government debt accumulation and the debt/GDP ratio is projected to fall to 53 per cent, comfortably below the Maastricht target. "Q2" also includes microeconomic reforms of the capital, labour and non-tradeable goods and services markets, and at the continuation of the privatisation programme.

The Government's programme aims at an improved policy mix. Up to 1992, monetary policy had borne the brunt of disinflation. The tightening of monetary conditions followed the abandonment of the regime of small, pre-announced currency depreciations in October 1990. High interest rates led to a considerable appreciation of the exchange rate, which was instrumental in reducing cost pressure, but put increasing strain on the open sector, while inflation in the sheltered sector remained high. Currency appreciation, however, was dampened by official intervention, manifest in a rapid build-up of international reserves. Domestic capital market reform accelerated and the shift towards indirect monetary control was completed. Up until mid-1992 restrictions on international capital inflows remained in place, but even with them it was difficult to keep liquidity growth on a sustainable path as foreign investment remained very high. The turnaround in inflation and the switch to a restrictive budgetary policy underpinned the April 1992 entry of the escudo in the ERM and the subsequent lifting of most capital controls. Keeping the exchange rate stable became the intermediate target of monetary policy and no new targets for liquidity growth have been specified for 1993. After the entry into the ERM of the European Monetary System, interest rates fell as strong capital inflows pushed the exchange rate temporarily towards the upper limit of the fluctuation band. In the second part of the year, however, conditions reversed, due not only to an easing of monetary policy, but also to growing tensions within the ERM. The escudo came under severe pressure in September 1992, and in November its central parity, along with that of the Spanish peseta, was reduced by 6 per cent. This episode did not lead to a change in the monetary policy stance and the Government has reiterated its commitment to a stable exchange rate as the anchor for disinflationary monetary policy. This will require a consistent policy framework.

Given the fixed parity and liberalised capital flows, which require monetary conditions to be set largely to manage the exchange rate, budgetary policy has become crucial to ensure a smooth path towards nominal convergence and to avoid distorting activity towards the sheltered sector at the expense of sectors engaged in international competition. Increasing inflationary pressure between 1989 and 1991 was fuelled by expansionary fiscal policy, with the deficit increasing from 3 to 6 per cent of GDP. Fiscal policy was put on a clear consolidation course in 1992. New budgetary objectives were defined in "Q2", focusing on a nominal primary expenditure target, which is binding for the State and indicative for the rest of the public sector. Budgetary restraint was significant, having been achieved by a further rise in the tax burden and an increase in primary expenditure, that was not higher than GDP growth. The cyclically-adjusted primary budget balance improved by 2 per cent of GDP. The overall deficit, however, fell by only 1 per cent to 5 per cent of GDP due to the cyclical slowdown and a sharp increase in spending on interest payments. The planned further move towards fiscal restraint in 1993 – the deficit is officially projected to fall to $4\frac{1}{4}$ per cent of GDP – relies upon tight control of primary spending, essentially public consumption, and a marked reduction in interest payments.

Since 1992 budgetary policy has not only become more ambitious in terms of reducing the government deficit but it has also put great emphasis on a shift to a new mode of fiscal consolidation, favouring expenditure cuts over tax increases. Such a shift was long overdue, as public expenditure had risen rapidly from very low levels over the past thirty years. Total expenditure reached 46.1 per cent of GDP in 1992, considerably above the OECD average and close to the European average; and, while the ratio of primary expenditure to GDP was close to the OECD average in 1992, it has continued to drift up over recent years. Thus, curbing primary spending has become a key ingredient in the government's strategy to promote fiscal convergence. Apart from specifying nominal expenditure ceilings, a new computerised monitoring system has been introduced, allowing overruns in specific areas to be quickly offset by spending cuts elsewhere.

Previous attempts to rein in public spending, while progressing quickly in some areas, had little success overall. Pay scales of civil servants were raised in 1989 so as to align them more closely with private sector wages. In addition, public employment increased, notably in the health and education sectors, notwithstanding efforts to upgrade the skills of existing public officials. As a result, public consumption rose from 16.1 per cent of GDP in 1989 to 18.2 per cent in 1992. Enforcing the strict expenditure ceilings announced in the 1993 Budget requires a substantial rise in job and geographical mobility in the public sector. New legislation has been adopted to this effect.

Welfare-related spending also surged during the 1980s, despite falling unemployment. Financing of the social security and National Health System (the latter largely financed by central government transfers) was relatively easy until the end of the 1980s, given revenue gains from brisk job creation. The public sector pay reform of 1989 entailed a sharp rise in payments to the National Health System. The authorities entered into negotiations in 1992 in order to strengthen the role of private health facilities. Payments of old-age pensions also increased rapidly, driven by improved benefit provisions and a structural shift to recipients of higher pension payments. The overall number of beneficiaries hardly changed. According to OECD calculations, demographic developments should not create too many financial problems over the next decade, but will entail a very rapid growth of expenditure thereafter. Reserves should thus be built up during the 1990s to create a sound financial base so that the pension system is able to meet heavy future obligations. One area where some progress in spending control has already been achieved is disability pensions, granted to an astonishingly high number of persons as a result of insufficient controls in the past. Thanks to tighter monitoring, the number of beneficiaries has begun to decline since 1989.

The Government also intends to improve public sector efficiency through the devolution of tasks to local authorities. This process has just started. Economic efficiency could be improved by a further devolution of tasks as decision making concerning the extent and quality of public services is brought closer to the beneficiaries. In order to ensure economy-wide gains, reforms need to be carefully designed, however: services provided at the local level should – as far as possible – be covered by charges and taxes at the local level; and central government administration should be reduced as responsibilities are passed to the local level.

Most progress in the reform of the public sector has been made in reducing government involvement in the business sector. It began to recede in the mid-1980s, ten years after the nationalisation wave. Government transfers to ailing enterprises fell from high levels and rapid progress was made in privatising public enterprises. Partial privatisation started in 1989, and full privatisation was allowed in 1990. By the end of 1992, cumulated proceeds from selling stakes in 25 enterprises amounted to about 6 per cent of 1992 GDP, a high figure by international comparison. Receipts of similar magnitude are expected over the three years to 1995. Even though debt take-overs accompanied privatisation, net proceeds have considerably slowed the accumulation of public debt. As a consequence, the gross public debt/GDP ratio dropped from a peak of 74 per cent GDP in 1988 to 65 per cent in 1992, a remarkable achievement. Besides cutting government aid to ailing state-owned enterprises and slowing debt accumulation, the privatisation process should enhance growth performance by improving efficiency in these enterprises and stimulating competition.

The high labour market flexibility observed in the past should be helpful in bearing on wage pressures. This flexibility is evidenced by the strong responsiveness of wage growth to changes in labour-market conditions and wage differentials that are large and also sensitive to market conditions. Wage agreements in the open sector have been considerably below those in the sheltered sector in the recent period. Nevertheless, a more rapid slowing of the momentum of wage increases would make the process of disinflation less costly. With this in mind, the Government is encouraging the conclusion of an income accord between the social partners which is compatible with its inflation objective and has led the way by granting civil service pay increases just at the lower end of its inflation target range. In addition, lowering barriers to lay offs would further enhance labour market flexibility and economic performance.

Structural policies have been strongly influenced by the implementation of the Single Market EC directives. Portugal is among the countries that have already incorporated most directives into domestic law. In addition, Portugal receives large transfers from the EC, geared mainly towards investment in still somewhat underdeveloped public infrastructure. Structural funds also aim at facilitating adjustment in the lagging agricultural sector, in industry, and in training and education. The government also intends to reduce the number of public monopolies and to liberalise the communication sector. Remaining barriers to competition in the sheltered sector, where inflation has remained stubbornly high, need to be removed, in order to reduce imbalances as the economy moves towards low inflation.

Joining the ERM and switching to fiscal restraint have made Portugal's anti-inflationary policies more credible. Important progress on the macroeconomic front has already been achieved, but full realisation of the convergence programme depends on the vigorous continuation of the current strategy. Structural reforms in recent years should help to reduce the costs of achieving nominal convergence in terms of output and employment losses. In pursuing their policy goals, the authorities are confronted with slow growth elsewhere in Europe, and growth in Portugal is likely to be sluggish over the next two years. However, in order to achieve full integration in the European Community and sustained growth, there is no option but to continue a firmly anchored monetary policy, fiscal consolidation emphasising control of expenditure and structural reforms.

Notes and references

1. The target range for inflation in 1993 was fixed at 5-7 per cent in the Budget, compared with 7-9 per cent for 1992.

2. Inflation is measured by the index of consumer prices, excluding rent.

3. The calculation of the effective exchange rate is based upon trade shares of 27 countries.

4. Differences for other spending categories are likely to be much smaller as price level differences are much less pronounced for private consumption and non-residential construction investment, the major component of government investment.

5. Total capital spending (including capital transfers) has progressed somewhat faster. Capital transfer data are only available on a net basis on a National Accounts basis in recent years. On a public accounts basis, capital transfers were about ²/₃ of investment. For France and Spain, the ratio was about half.

6. Between 1991 and mid-1992, the central bank used Treasury bills for purposes of absorbing liquidity. This operation, while having an effect on gross debt and gross interest payments, left net stocks and flows unaffected.

7. With the abolition of frontier controls, VAT for EC-trade is no longer collected immediately at the frontier, but is collected later following the sale on the domestic market.

8. There is a counterpart to this operation on the revenue side, inducing a fall in property income of the government.

9. In its efforts to soak up liquidity since April 1991, the Bank of Portugal has used money markets to reduce bank liquidity through repurchases of Treasury bills and other financial instruments (money market intervention rate or regular liquidity draining rate). At that time, it also introduced a lending rate (rate of regular provision of liquidity) See, *OECD Economic Survey of Portugal, 1991/1992.*

10. Portuguese bank charges continue to be among the highest in Europe. See: *The Economist,* 14th November 1992, p. 87.

11. Banco de Portugal (1993), Monthly Bulletin, No. 1, January, p. VII.

12. A.C. Leal and J. Ramalho (1993), ''Politica e situacao monetarias no segundo semestre de 1992'', Bank of Portugal, pp. 34-35.

13. In September 1992, with turbulence on foreign exchange markets driving short-term capital out of the country, the Bank of Portugal suspended its regular interventions in the domestic money market. ''Regular draining'' of liquidity resumed in October via issues of the Central

Bank's monetary certificates at a rate of 14 per cent. In the face of renewed exchange rate pressures, it was suspended for a week beginning on 26 November. Transactions for the "regular provision of liquidity" have been kept in abeyance since September 1992.

14. Part I of the last Survey described in some detail major changes due to EC accession.

15. The trend decline in the saving ratio since 1986 may also have been influenced by structural changes since EC accession, notably an increase in expected permanent income (wealth effect), the progressive waning of liquidity constraints due to financial-market deregulation and, until 1991, the sharp rise in retirement pensions.

16. The quarterly labour force survey was modified in 1992. The household sample was modified on the basis of the results of the 1991 Census of the population. In addition, the minimum age for entering the labour force was raised from 13 to 15 years. In 1991, the 13-15 age group represented 0.6 per cent of total employment. Comparisons between labour-market developments in 1992 and earlier years might thus be misleading, notably for the younger age brackets.

17. The share in total employees of those working less than 25 hours a week rose from 7.6 per cent in 1989 to 8.8 per cent in 1991, and to an estimated 9 per cent in 1992.

18. Hourly productivity rose by ½ a per cent in 1991 and an estimated 2 to 2½ per cent in 1992.

19. In the absence of any official gap-bridging estimates, the Secretariat assumed that the change in definitions probably lowered the unemployment rate by 0.3-0.4 percentage points.

20. Adding those unemployed who have not "actively" sought employment for over a month to numbers unemployed in the quarterly labour force survey would raise the unemployment rate to 5.7 per cent of the labour force.

21. Numerous *caveats* affect labour market statistics in Portugal.

22. According to the 1991 Census. On the basis of the 1981 Census and subsequent changes, employment in agriculture would still amount to 17 per cent of total employment in 1991.

23. The coverage ratio is to be compared with rates of over 90 per cent in Canada, 80 per cent in the United Kingdom, 60 per cent in Germany, 57 per cent in France and 30 per cent in the United States.

24. Banco de Portugal (1992), "Deflator da procura e taxa de cambio real: Desagregacao por custos de producao", Boletim trimestral, September.

25. The Gulf war adversely affected exports of energy-intensive products, notably chemicals.

26. Imported inputs account for about half the total inputs in exports.

27. According to the Bank of Portugal, the ratio of the private domestic demand price deflator to merchandise import prices rose by some 70 per cent between mid-1989 and the end of 1992.

28. The results of the tourism sector have been worsening over the past five years. Average daily spending by tourists has been falling, and the average stay has decreased from 10.4 days to 7.4 days. At the same time the rate of growth of touristic capacity rose by 21 per cent a year.

Annex I

Bibliography

BORGES, A. and D.F.H. DE LUCENA (1988), "Social security in Portugal: a system in disequilibrium", in A. de Sousa (ed.), *Nova Economia em Portugal,* Universidade Nova de Lisboa.

BRAGA DE MACEDO J. (1990), External liberalization with ambiguous public response: the experience of Portugal, Working Paper No. 138, Universidade Nova de Lisboa.

COHN, E. and J. COSTA (1986), "Equity and efficiency effects of intergovernmental aid: the case of Portugal", *Public Finance* Vol. XXXXI, No. 1.

COURAKIS, A.S., F.M. ROQUE and G. TRIDIMAS (1990), "Public expenditure growth in Greece and Portugal: Wagner's law and beyond", Working Paper No. 146, Universidade Nova de Lisboa.

GASPAR V. and A. M. PEREIRA (1992), "A dynamic general equilibrium analysis of EC structural funds (with an application to Portugal)", Working Paper No. 191, Universidade Nova de Lisboa (July).

KATZ, L.F. and A.B. KRUEGER (1992), "Flexibilité des rémunérations dans lesecteur public: la situation du marché du travail et les considérations budgétaires", Colloque sur la flexibilité des rémunérations dans le secteur public, OCDE/GD(92)158, Paris.

MINISTRY OF FINANCE (1992), "Analise do sector publico administrativo e empresarial em 1991", GAFEEP, Lisboa.

MODESTO, L., M.L MONTEIRO and J.C. NEVES (1992): "Some Aspects of the Portuguese Labour Market, 1977-88: Neutrality, Hysteresis and the Wage gap", in *The Portuguese Economy towards 1992,* Boston.

OECD (1992), *OECD Economic Survey of Portugal, 1991/1992,* Paris.

OECD (1993), "Pension liabilities in the seven major economies", Working Party No. 1 of the Economic Policy Committee (COM/ECO/DIV/PUMA/SBO(93)5).

OECD (1993*a*), "1992-1993 Annual Review-Iceland-Annexes", ECO/EDR(93)8/ANN1/²/₃.

ORVALHO, J. and J. NABAIS (1990), "Portugal: La gestion des ressources humaines. La phase du changement", *Revue francaise d'administration publique,* No. 55 (juillet-septembre).

OXLEY, H., M. MAHER, J.P. MARTIN, G. NICOLETTI and P. ALONSO-GAMO (1990), "The public sector: Issues for the 1990s", OECD Economics and Statistics Department Working Papers No. 90 (December).

OWEN, J.P. (1989), "Financing lower tiers of Government: a European perspective", *Intertax*, 1989/12.

PINTO BARBOSA, A.S. (1992), Fiscal decentralization: the Portuguese Case, Universidade Nova de Lisboa, mimeo, (December).

SCHULTZE, C.L. (1992), "Is there a bias toward excess in U.S. government budgets and deficits?" *Journal of Economic Perspectives*, Vol. 6, No. 2 (Spring).

VON HAGEN, J. (1992), "Budgeting procedures and fiscal performance in the European Communities", EC Economic Papers No. 96, (October).

Annex II

Supplementary table and diagram

Table A1. **Government revenue and expenditure trends**

Per cent of GDP

	1985	1986	1987	1988	1989	1990	1991	1992[1]
Total receipts	35.9	37.6	36.2	38.1	38.7	37.9	38.6	41.0
Total direct taxes	8.9	7.3	6.2	7.7	9.4	9.3	10.2	11.1
Households	6.9	5.6	4.2	5.4	6.6	6.0	6.8	7.3
Business	1.9	1.7	2.0	2.3	2.8	3.3	3.4	3.9
Current transfers received	10.6	11.2	12.6	12.3	12.2	11.6	11.8	12.2
Indirect taxes	15.1	17.4	15.6	16.7	15.5	15.4	14.7	15.7
Property and entrepreneurial income	1.3	1.7	1.8	1.4	1.6	1.6	1.8	2.0
Total expenditure	43.5	44.0	43.5	43.5	41.9	42.9	44.7	46.1
Government consumption	15.5	15.4	15.2	16.0	16.1	16.7	17.7	18.2
Debt interest	9.3	9.7	8.8	7.8	7.1	8.1	8.4	9.0
Subsidies	3.6	3.0	1.9	1.8	1.5	1.3	1.6	1.4
Social-security outlays	9.0	9.1	9.4	9.7	9.5	9.5	9.5	9.3
Other current transfers paid	2.0	3.3	3.8	3.7	3.6	3.8	3.8	3.7
Current disbursements, total	39.5	40.5	39.1	39.0	37.8	39.4	40.9	41.6
Saving	-3.5	-2.9	-2.9	-0.9	0.9	-1.4	-2.3	-0.6
Gross investment	3.1	3.3	3.3	3.6	3.5	3.4	3.7	4.2
Net capital transfers received	-0.8	-0.2	-1.0	-0.8	-0.6	-0.1	-0.0	-0.2
Net lending	-7.5	-6.4	-7.3	-5.4	-3.2	-5.0	-6.1	-5.1

1. OECD estimates.
Sources: OECD, *National Accounts* and estimates.

Diagram A1. **WELFARE PAYMENTS AND BENEFICIARIES**
Index 1985 = 100

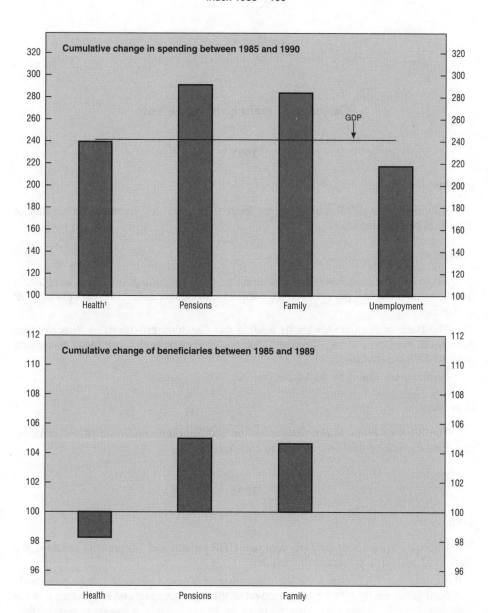

1. Welfare payments related to sickness and maternity.
Source: National Institute of Statistics.

Annex III

Calendar of main economic events

1991

October

Adoption of legislation aligning the legal framework for youth labour on that of mass European countries.

November

Adoption of a new convergence programme ("Q2"), aiming, *inter alia,* at reducing the rate of inflation to 4 per cent and the public-sector budget deficit to 3 per cent of GDP by 1995.

The Bank of Portugal lowers its lending rate (liquidity provision) by $\frac{1}{4}$ percentage point to 20 per cent and its "draining" rate on the money-market rate by $\frac{1}{8}$ percentage point to $15\frac{5}{8}$ per cent.

Pensions are raised by 12-14 per cent.

December

The Bank of Portugal extends the ban on acquisition by non-residents of variable-rate domestic public-debt instruments to end-April 1992.

1992

January

Under the assumption of 3 per cent real GDP growth and 7-9 per cent inflation, the draft 1992 budget is presented. It includes:

– Reform of the VAT system *via* the imposition of a new 5 per cent rate on previously 0-rated goods partly offset by the removal of the 8 per cent rate and the lowering of the standard rate to 16 per cent. Specific taxes on goods, notably vehicles, were modified;
– Introduction of a nominal primary-expenditure ceiling, with increased spending on health and education to be partly offset by a freeze in other areas.

This would allow the deficit to fall from 6.3 per cent of GDP in 1991 to 5.2 per cent in 1992.

The Bank of Portugal sets a target growth rate of 12 per cent for L- in 1992.

February

Privatisation of the remaining 60 per cent public stake in BESCL, the country's third largest bank (yielding Esc 89 billion).

The Bank of Portugal modifies procedures for "occasional" interventions in the money market.

The Bank of Portugal lowers its lending rate by $\frac{1}{2}$ a percentage point to $19\frac{1}{2}$ per cent.

Incomes policy agreement, signed by the Government and the social partners, aims at holding nominal wage increases to 10.8 per cent in the first quarter, 9.8 per cent in the second quarter and 8.5 per cent in the following 3 months.

March

The Bank of Portugal lowers its lending rate by 9/16 percentage point to 18 15/16 per cent.

The Bank of Portugal reduces the deposit required on domestic firms' non-trade foreign currency borrowing from 40 per cent to 30 per cent.

April

The escudo joins the exchange-rate mechanism of the EMS, with a central rate of 178.135 escudos per ecu and a fluctuation band of 6 per cent around the central rate.

The minimum wage is raised by 11 per cent to Esc 44 500 and by 13.4 per cent to Esc 38 000 for household services. Most pension and social-security benefits are raised by 10 per cent.

The Bank of Portugal lowers its lending rate by 1 percentage point to 17 15/16 per cent and its "draining" rate by $\frac{1}{4}$ percentage point to $15\frac{3}{8}$ per cent.

The Bank of Portugal extends the ban on acquisition by non-residents of variable-rate domestic public-debt instruments until end-year.

Full privatisation of the insurance company *Mundial Confiança* (yielding Esc. 33.4 billion).

May

The minimum rate for time deposits from 180 days up to a year and the rate on demand deposits are liberalised.

Privatisation of 17.6 per cent of *Banco Português do Atlantico* (yielding Esc 50.6 billion).

June

Privatisation of 25 per cent of the largest oil company Petrogal (yielding Esc 40.8 billion).

Reform of public accounting procedures aiming at better spending control.

July

The Bank of Portugal reduces the deposit required on domestic firms' non-trade foreign currency borrowing from 30 to 25 per cent.

The Bank of Portugal lowers its lending rate by 3/16 percentage point to 17¾ per cent and its "draining" rate by ⅛ percentage point to 15¼ per cent.

The right to strike is changed: a new law extends the minimum service provisions to workers in the energy, transportation, mining and public health sectors.

August

The Bank of Portugal liberalises the purchase by residents of foreign securities and discontinues the issuing of Treasury bills for the purpose of money-market management.

The Bank of Portugal abolishes the deposit required on domestic firms' non-trade foreign currency borrowing. Non-residents are allowed to buy floating-rate government bonds (this facility had been suspended in July 1991).

The Bank of Portugal lowers its lending rate in two steps (by ¾ and 1 percentage point) to 16 per cent and its "draining" rate (by ¼ and 1 percentage point) to 14 per cent.

Creation of new short-term debt instrument: The "Commercial Paper".

September

Residents are allowed to borrow abroad.

The Bank of Portugal reduces the amounts domestic banks can lend on the Euro-escudo market by two-thirds.

The Bank of Portugal suspends "regular" interventions into the money market and, as well, "liquidity-providing" operations.

October

Under the assumption of 3 per cent real GDP growth and 7½ per cent inflation, the draft 1993 budget aims at reducing the public-sector deficit to 4.2 per cent of GDP. As in 1992, a binding ceiling on primary expenditure is imposed, which implies a slight increase in real total public spending in 1993, with health and defence outlays rising faster.

Extension of the definition of redundant employment to public-sector workers affected by the disappearance of government services and entities, and by changes in required qualifications.

Changes in both lay-off legislation and legal framework governing collective labour contracts aim at making labour markets more flexible.

Rules for monitoring applications for health benefits are tightened.

November

The central rate of the escudo against other currencies of the ERM is adjusted downwards by 6 per cent to Esc. 182.194 per ECU.

Full privatisation of the insurance company *Imperio* (yielding Esc. 25.5 billion).

Pensions are raised by 6.5 to 8.4 per cent.

December

The Parliament ratifies the Maastricht Treaty. The Treasury overdraft facility with the central bank is abolished.

Full liberalisation of all external borrowings by residents, regardless of their nature or maturity.

During wage negotiations between employers and trade unions, the Government declares that salary increases of more than 6 per cent (the mid-point in the 5-7 per cent inflation target) in the private sector in 1993 must be avoided, and that wages [] in the public sector will be raised by no more than 5 to 5½ per cent. Similar guidelines apply to public enterprises.

Adoption of legislation seeking to enhance labour mobility in public administration.

Full privatisation of the bank *Credito Predial Português* (yielding Esc 40.8 billion).

Adoption of new banking law, strengthening prudential surveillance (supervision on a consolidated basis) and putting into effect provisions of the EC Second Banking Co-ordination Directive.

Publication of the "State Budget Law for 1993", providing for tighter controls of primary spending in line with "Q2", the Convergence Programme adopted in November 1991.

1993

January

All remaining controls on foreigners' access to the short-term domestic money market are lifted by the Bank of Portugal.

Issue of 5-year bonds of the Portuguese Republic on Euro-market, the first international issue in four years.

The Bank of Portugal lowers its "draining" rate by 1 percentage point to 13 per cent.

New legislation gives greater role to the private sector in supplying health services.

February

Privatisation of 61 per cent of the bank *União de Bancos Portugueses.*

The Bank of Portugal lowers its "draining" rate by ¼ of a percentage point to 12¾ per cent.

Social security benefits are raised by 6 per cent, the mid-point of the 5 to 7 per cent target range for inflation.

March

The minimum wage is raised by 6.5 per cent to ESC 47 400 and by 7.5 per cent to Esc 41 000 for household services.

The Bank of Portugal raises its "draining" rate to 13.5 per cent.

Annex IV

The size of government: some contributory factors

An econometric attempt to evaluate the aggregate level of primary government spending in international comparison was presented in Part II. This Annex provides some further results. Usually, demand for public services are thought to depend on the same factors as demand for private goods: preferences, income and relative prices. In addition, demographics are likely to influence demand for certain age-specific services. As well as population density, which serves as a proxy for increased costs due to urbanisation, the size of population may also play a role, as there could be economies of scale in the provision of some public services. Preferences and institutional features are also important, although difficult to capture empirically. The attempt by Jurgen von Hagen (1992) to embody budgeting procedures in a single index is mentioned in the Survey, but data are only available for the EC.

The specification of cross-country equations closely follows Schultze (1992). The data are based on decade averages for 19 OECD countries.* The results presented in Table 4 in the main text are similar to Schultze's with respect to demographic variables and population size and density. The share of the population above 65 years has quite a strong effect on spending, while it is difficult to find any effect for cohorts below 15 years. The size of the population has some positive impact, while density has a slightly negative effect. Where results differ, however, is with respect to the income elasticity and the role of relative prices. In order to estimate the income elasticity, Schultze includes *per capita* GDP as measured by PPP's and finds income elasticities ranging from 1.3 to 1.6 for different specifications of his basic equation. However, his left-hand side variable, the ratio of government spending to GDP is not measured in international prices.

While GDP numbers in PPP's are readily available, data for government expenditure are not. As a proxy, price levels for government consumption are related here to the U.S. price level, in the same way as prices in any country are related to a reference country in order to construct the numbers for international comparisons of real GDP. The coefficient on this variable is close to one in the regression results reported in Table 4. The following

---

* Iceland, Turkey, Luxembourg, Greece and Switzerland are excluded, because of the unavailability of information.

	Primary expenditure/GDP ratio					
Population above 65 years	0.70	(4.5)	0.74	5.1)	0.71	(4.9)
Population below 15 years	−0.04	(-0.2)	−0.01	(-0.1)	0.05	(0.3)
Population size	−0.07	(-3.6)	−0.04	(-2.9)	−0.06	(-3.2)
Population density	0.01	(1.0)	0.03	(2.0)	0.03	(2.1)
GDP (PPP) per capita	0.11	(2.4)	..		0.06	(1.5)
Relative price effect	..		0.23	(3.2)	0.19	(2.5)
R_2	0.71		0.74		0.75	
	Primary expenditure/PPP GDP ratio					
SEE	0.11		0.11		0.10	
Population above 65 years	0.60	(1.8)	0.65	(4.3)	0.61	(4.1)
Population below 15 years	−0.29	(-0.7)	0.05	(0.3)	0.11	(0.6)
Population size	−0.16	(-3.7)	−0.08	(-5.7)	−0.11	(-5.4)
Population density	−0.02	(-0.5)	0.06	(3.9)	0.06	(4.1)
GDP (PPP) per capita	0.28	(2.8)	..		0.08	(1.8)
Relative price effect	..		0.96	(12.6)	0.91	(11.5)
R_2	0.51		0.90		0.90	
SEE	0.24		0.11		0.11	

Note: Data are in logs. T-statistics are in parenthesis.

table summarises results for different combinations of left-hand side and right-hand side variables:

A significant effect of *per capita* GDP can be found in the equations which do not include a relative price effect. Even then it is smaller than found by Schultze. Including relative prices the income elasticity is somewhat above, but never significantly different from one.

A unitary income elasticity does not rule out that certain public goods are luxuries, as found for health expenditure in OECD (1993a), while other expenditure items expand less fast than income. Based on time-series analysis (for the period 1958 to 1985), Courakis *et. al.* (1990) find elasticities for Portuguese government investment and transfers, which are close to unity, while that for government consumption is larger than one, but still much smaller than Schultze's low estimate.

STATISTICAL AND STRUCTURAL ANNEX

Selected background statistics

	Average 1982-91	1982	1983	1984	1985	1986	1987	1988	1989	1990	1991
A. Percentage changes											
Private consumption[1]	3.0	2.4	-1.4	-2.9	0.7	5.6	5.4	6.6	3.3	5.3	5.2
Government consumption[1]	3.9	3.7	3.8	0.2	6.4	7.2	4.9	5.3	2.8	1.5	3.0
Gross fixed capital formation[1]	2.4	2.3	-7.1	-17.4	-3.5	10.9	15.1	15.0	5.6	5.9	2.5
Total domestic demand[1]	2.9	2.2	-5.7	-6.7	0.9	8.3	10.4	7.4	4.3	5.4	4.1
Exports of goods and services[1]	8.5	4.7	13.6	11.6	6.7	6.8	8.6	10.2	13.3	9.5	1.1
Imports of goods and services[1]	6.8	3.9	-6.1	-4.4	1.4	16.9	20.0	16.1	9.1	10.1	4.9
GDP[1]	2.8	2.1	-0.2	-1.9	2.8	4.1	5.3	3.9	5.2	4.4	2.2
GDP price deflator	17.5	20.7	24.7	24.5	21.8	20.4	11.3	11.6	13.0	14.3	13.6
Industrial production	4.6	7.8	3.6	2.3	0.9	7.3	4.3	3.6	7.0	9.2	0.0
Employment	1.6	-0.1	3.9	-0.1	-0.5	0.2	2.6	2.6	2.2	2.2	3.0
Compensation of employees (current prices)	19.2	22.1	21.8	18.2	20.7	20.0	18.8	14.5	15.3	21.0	19.2
Productivity (real GDP/employment)	1.1	2.2	-4.0	-1.8	3.3	3.9	2.6	1.3	2.9	2.1	-0.7
Unit labour costs (compensation/real GDP)	15.9	19.5	22.1	20.5	17.4	15.2	12.9	10.2	9.7	15.9	16.7
B. Percentage ratios											
Gross fixed capital formation as percent of GDP at constant prices	26.4	29.7	27.6	23.2	21.8	23.2	25.4	28.1	28.2	28.6	28.7
Stockbuilding as percent of GDP at constant prices	1.5	3.3	-0.9	-1.6	-1.2	0.2	3.2	2.4	2.9	3.4	3.4
Foreign balance as percent of GDP at constant prices	-13.2	-18.0	-11.5	-6.0	-4.1	-8.2	-13.5	-17.3	-16.3	-17.4	-19.6
Compensation of employees as percent of GDP at current prices	47.2	52.0	50.9	49.3	47.5	45.5	46.1	45.6	44.2	44.9	46.1
Direct taxes as percent of household income	5.7	5.1	6.1	5.7	6.1	5.3	4.0	5.2	6.5	5.9	6.6
Household saving as percent of disposable income	25.4	28.4	26.7	27.7	28.7	26.3	25.6	22.3	22.4	23.3	22.3
Unemployment rate[2]	6.8	7.5	7.8	8.5	8.7	8.6	7.2	5.8	5.1	4.7	4.1
C. Other indicator											
Current balance (billion dollars)	-0.4	-3.1	-0.8	-0.6	0.4	1.2	0.5	-1.0	0.2	-0.1	-0.7

1. At constant 1985 prices.
2. Data based on the narrowest definition of unemployment.
Sources: National Institute of Statistics (INE); Bank of Portugal; OECD estimates.

Table A. Expenditure on gross domestic product

Billion escudos

	1981	1982	1983	1984	1985	1986	1987	1988	1989	1990	1991
A. At current prices											
Private consumption	1 040.2	1 280.3	1 589.3	1 981.0	2 380.3	2 860.7	3 318.8	3 890.7	4 504.7	5 340.6	6 297.1
Government consumption	231.2	284.0	360.4	432.6	559.4	693.8	803.5	977.6	1 168.7	1 445.8	1 696.0
Gross fixed investment	463.0	574.8	671.5	663.7	768.0	977.0	1 250.8	1 611.2	1 885.0	2 243.3	2 574.9
Stockbuilding	55.8	56.4	-20.8	-37.7	-40.8	10.6	171.0	169.8	192.2	231.2	231.2
Total domestic demand	1 790.2	2 195.5	2 600.4	3 039.5	3 666.9	4 542.1	5 544.1	6 649.3	7 750.6	9 260.9	10 799.2
Exports	389.6	487.5	719.3	1 047.5	1 315.2	1 465.8	1 773.7	2 126.2	2 670.5	3 100.7	3 165.5
Imports	678.5	832.6	1 016.2	1 272.8	1 458.6	1 590.0	2 144.4	2 774.5	3 292.8	3 858.7	4 094.7
GDP (at market prices)	1 501.2	1 850.4	2 303.4	2 814.1	3 523.4	4 417.9	5 173.4	6 001.0	7 128.3	8 503.0	9 870.0
Net factor income from abroad	-61.0	-103.0	-119.6	-177.3	-196.4	-151.6	-130.8	-125.8	-113.1	-34.1	2.8
GNP (at market prices)	1 440.2	1 747.4	2 183.8	2 636.8	3 327.0	4 266.3	5 042.6	5 875.2	7 015.2	8 468.9	9 872.8
B. At 1985 prices											
Private consumption	2 427.8	2 484.9	2 449.3	2 377.2	2 393.2	2 527.0	2 663.1	2 838.3	2 932.1	3 088.0	3 249.8
Government consumption	476.3	494.0	512.7	513.9	546.9	586.1	614.6	647.2	665.0	674.7	694.9
Gross fixed investment	1 014.9	1 037.8	963.8	796.2	768.0	851.4	979.7	1 126.3	1 189.8	1 260.4	1 291.9
Stockbuilding	122.4	114.2	-31.7	-54.2	-40.8	6.1	125.3	96.0	121.7	150.8	151.0
Total domestic demand	4 041.4	4 130.9	3 894.1	3 633.0	3 667.3	3 970.7	4 382.7	4 707.9	4 908.6	5 173.9	5 387.7
Exports	928.9	972.2	1 104.5	1 233.0	1 315.2	1 404.1	1 525.0	1 680.2	1 903.4	2 084.1	2 107.8
Imports	1 544.0	1 603.7	1 505.2	1 438.3	1 458.6	1 704.8	2 045.1	2 374.0	2 591.0	2 852.4	2 992.2
GDP (at market prices)	3 426.3	3 499.4	3 493.4	3 427.7	3 523.9	3 669.9	3 862.6	4 014.1	4 221.0	4 405.6	4 503.2

Sources: National Institute of Statistics (INE); Bank of Portugal; OECD estimates.

Table B. **Household appropriation account**

Billion escudos

	1982	1983	1984	1985	1986	1987	1988	1989	1990	1991
Compensation of employees	963.0	1 173.3	1 386.8	1 674.0	2 008.9	2 386.6	2 733.8	3 153.4	3 816.2	4 550.5
Property and entrepreneurial income	719.1	923.6	1 229.9	1 552.4	1 686.5	1 795.9	2 047.4	2 504.2	2 956.8	3 429.8
Domestic transfers	241.4	294.6	361.3	440.1	595.9	763.6	881.3	1 021.6	1 242.6	1 476.7
Foreign transfers	215.0	242.0	320.3	358.3	395.6	479.9	520.6	587.9	637.9	695.3
Gross total income	2 138.5	2 633.5	3 298.3	4 024.8	4 686.9	5 426.0	6 183.1	7 267.1	8 653.5	10 152.3
Direct taxes	108.9	161.3	188.6	244.8	249.0	218.1	324.0	468.9	512.2	672.1
Social security contributions	241.6	305.1	372.0	440.5	555.1	746.2	850.9	989.5	1 179.0	1 378.3
Disposable income	1 788.0	2 167.1	2 737.7	3 339.5	3 882.7	4 461.7	5 008.1	5 808.7	6 962.3	8 101.9
Consumption	1 280.9	1 587.6	1 980.4	2 381.4	2 861.8	3 320.0	3 891.6	4 505.7	5 341.9	6 298.7
Savings ratio[1]	28.4	26.7	27.7	28.7	26.3	25.6	22.3	22.4	23.3	22.3
Real disposable income percentage change	2.5	–3.8	–1.6	2.2	2.1	4.4	2.0	3.5	6.5	3.9

1. As a percentage of disposable income.
Sources: Ministry of Finance; Bank of Portugal; OECD estimates.

101

Table C. General government account

Billion escudos

	1982	1983	1984	1985	1986	1987	1988	1989	1990	1991
Current receipts	654.4	869.2	1 051.1	1 266.7	1 660.2	1 873.2	2 285.6	2 756.1	3 196.4	3 802.4
Direct taxes	146.9	206.7	246.7	313.3	322.0	319.4	463.3	668.0	764.6	1 002.5
Social security contributions	194.9	244.6	298.5	354.0	449.2	602.1	691.3	797.0	949.8	1 139.8
Indirect taxes	275.4	358.5	436.8	534.2	767.9	804.8	1 002.8	1 104.5	1 308.8	1 435.9
Capital income	26.7	47.7	54.2	46.2	76.9	95.4	83.2	114.8	137.1	181.0
Other current receipts	10.5	11.8	14.9	19.1	44.2	51.4	45.1	71.8	36.1	43.3
Current expenditure	669.3	835.4	1 085.0	1 389.5	1 787.4	2 023.9	2 342.0	2 683.7	3 347.4	4 114.4
Expenditure on goods and services	276.2	348.4	423.1	546.9	678.8	787.8	962.2	1 147.4	1 422.8	1 741.7
Subsidies	79.6	91.8	120.1	127.1	131.1	98.4	109.5	105.5	106.5	120.3
Interest paid	97.9	141.4	231.0	329.0	428.1	453.0	467.6	507.4	692.3	832.2
Current transfers	215.6	253.8	310.7	386.5	549.4	684.7	802.7	923.3	1 125.8	1 420.2
Saving	-14.9	33.9	-33.8	-122.8	-127.2	-150.7	-56.4	72.5	-151.0	-312.0
Capital expenditure	125.6	266.7	163.1	137.2	151.9	224.4	267.9	287.7	299.0	357.9
Fixed investment	79.9	88.6	90.7	108.9	144.0	170.9	216.9	246.1	290.9	350.6
Transfers	45.7	178.1	72.4	28.3	8.0	53.5	50.9	41.6	8.1	7.3
Overall balance	-141.1	-233.1	-198.4	-261.3	-281.5	-377.9	-326.8	-218.3	-453.9	-674.6
(as a percentage of GDP)	-7.6	-10.1	-7.1	-7.4	-6.4	-7.3	-5.4	-3.1	-5.3	-6.8
Loans	25.9	30.9	39.3	37.1	78.0	107.5	82.2	97.9	98.0	47.0
Total borrowing requirement	-167.0	-264.0	-237.7	-298.4	-359.5	-485.4	-409.0	-316.2	-551.9	-721.6
(as a percentage of GDP)	-9.0	-11.5	-8.4	-8.5	-8.1	-9.4	-6.8	-4.4	-6.5	-7.3

Sources: OECD, *National Accounts*; Ministry of Finance; OECD estimates.

Table D. **Prices and wages**
Percentage changes

	1982	1983	1984	1985	1986	1987	1988	1989	1990	1991
Consumer prices[1]										
Total[2]	22.4	25.5	29.3	19.3	11.7	9.4	9.6	12.6	13.4	11.4
Food and drink	24.1	25.1	30.8	17.7	9.1	8.8	9.2	14.4	13.6	9.9
Clothing and footwear	15.6	19.8	24.4	23.3	23.5	15.8	13.2	10.5	9.5	11.9
Housing costs	20.1	29.0	33.8	20.0	10.7	7.4	10.1	11.8	11.9	12.1
Miscellaneous	22.7	27.8	24.7	21.9	14.5	9.0	6.0	11.6	11.3	10.9
Wages in manufacturing industry										
Nominal[3]	20.5	18.7	18.8	21.1	16.8	14.0	11.3	14.8	16.2	16.4
Real[3]	-1.5	-5.4	-7.8	1.2	4.5	4.2	1.5	2.0	2.5	4.5

1. Mainland. New index as from 1988.
2. Excluding rent.
3. Break in series in 1990.
Sources: INE; Bank of Portugal; OECD, *Main Economic Indicators.*

Table E. Civilian employment by sector[1]
Thousands

	1982	1983	1984	1985	1986	1987	1988	1989	1990	1991
Agriculture	991.0	957.0	969.0	969.0	891.0	926.0	885.0	829.0	795.0	799.0
Mining	25.0	28.3	28.2	28.3	27.0	27.0	29.0	20.0	19.0	14.0
Manufacturing	1 016.0	1 458.0	1 388.0	1 377.0	995.0	1 040.0	1 074.0	1 107.0	1 127.0	1 151.0
Construction	412.0	298.8	305.7	328.3	332.0	354.0	362.0	384.0	376.0	381.0
Electricity, gas and water	19.0	44.4	39.7	34.8	32.0	33.0	38.0	38.0	45.0	54.0
Transport and communication	160.0	190.2	187.5	179.8	174.0	168.0	177.0	180.0	201.0	216.0
Trade	470.0	659.7	638.6	610.5	599.0	585.0	630.0	655.0	679.0	728.0
Banking, insurance, real estate	97.0	134.7	135.0	131.9	127.0	132.0	140.0	154.0	205.0	218.0
Personal services	737.0	883.5	889.7	885.2	887.0	906.0	945.0	1 009.0	1 025.0	1 045.0
Total	3 927.0	4 654.6	4 581.4	4 544.8	4 064.0	4 171.0	4 280.0	4 376.0	4 472.0	4 606.0

1. New series as from 1983.
Sources: OECD, Labour Force Statistics and OECD estimates.

Table F. **Money supply and its counterparts**

Billion escudos at end of period

	1982	1983	1984	1985	1986	1987	1988	1989	1990	1991
Total money supply (L)	2 199.0	2 650.3	3 385.8	4 310.7	5 280.3	6 045.1	6 892.6	7 552.7	8 883.0	10 646.2
Money (M1-)	610.5	666.3	772.4	980.8	1 334.3	1 526.5	1 722.1	1 827.8	2 352.2	2 704.9
Notes and coins in circulation	219.5	240.1	267.3	319.0	399.3	457.7	509.5	577.3	623.9	683.1
Sight deposits of households and enterprises	391.0	426.2	505.1	661.8	935.0	1 068.8	1 212.6	1 250.5	1 728.3	2 021.8
Quasi money[1]	1 588.5	1 984.0	2 613.4	3 329.9	3 946.0	4 518.6	5 170.5	5 724.9	6 530.8	7 941.3
Counterparts										
Net foreign assets	470.7	565.9	773.7	972.6	935.1	1 180.5	1 826.6	2 511.9	2 715.5	3 446.8
Net lending to the public sector	495.6	654.1	900.6	1 348.7	1 865.5	2 332.2	2 616.0	2 545.5	2 796.5	2 758.1
Lending to the private sector	1 675.3	2 102.5	2 545.8	2 785.3	3 097.2	3 199.7	3 525.5	3 703.8	4 981.5	6 284.0
Miscellaneous, net	-442.6	-672.2	-834.3	-795.9	-617.5	-667.3	-1 075.5	-1 208.5	-1 610.5	-1 842.7

1. Including migrant deposits and Treasury bills.
Source: Bank of Portugal, *Quarterly Bulletin.*

Table G. **Breakdown by nationality of foreign visitors**

Thousands

	1982	1983	1984	1985	1986	1987	1988	1989	1990	1991
Total	7 299.3	8 875.0	9 811.0	11 691.7	13 056.9	16 173.3	16 076.7	16 470.9	18 422.1	19 641.3
Spain	5 173.3	6 512.6	7 308.8	8 798.2	9 960.2	12 583.3	12 124.4	12 185.9	13 806.3	14 583.2
United Kingdom	570.6	629.5	709.7	880.4	1 069.1	1 204.3	1 139.7	1 137.3	1 202.9	1 307.3
Germany	289.5	355.3	344.0	413.0	430.3	526.0	568.7	611.0	681.0	851.9
France	288.4	327.9	326.6	347.3	350.1	434.8	593.4	646.4	658.2	711.5
Netherlands	124.7	156.2	151.9	163.8	171.7	214.2	285.2	332.7	329.5	360.5
United States	154.2	186.8	209.4	229.5	149.8	195.1	223.3	234.7	252.1	178.1
Italy	72.5	66.1	71.8	93.4	108.5	134.4	154.7	185.1	221.1	291.0
Brazil	80.2	57.4	60.2	69.2	82.5	71.7	92.1	102.4	118.9	114.1
Canada	42.0	46.8	56.1	70.3	73.8	77.5	79.1	90.9	90.8	69.3
Sweden	71.1	65.5	71.5	54.1	69.4	70.1	86.5	94.7	97.6	114.3
Belgium	48.6	61.4	59.1	67.6	67.7	90.3	116.9	150.7	173.1	198.4
Switzerland	41.2	46.1	53.2	61.1	66.4	70.6	73.3	77.7	78.0	79.9
Other countries	343.0	363.4	388.7	443.9	457.3	501.5	539.5	621.3	712.7	781.9

Source: INE, *Boletim mensal de estatística.*

106

Table H. Foreign trade by main commodity groups

Million US dollars and percentages

	1982	1983	1984	1985	1986	1987	1988	1989	1990	1991
Imports, total (Million $)	9 540.7	8 256.7	7 975.3	7 649.7	9 454.0	13 965.7	17 884.8	19 043.1	25 332.6	26 328.6
As a percentage of total										
Food and beverages	11.3	10.7	11.5	11.0	11.0	10.6	10.3	9.9	9.7	11.2
Basic material and semi-finished goods	35.9	37.1	42.3	39.1	25.0	19.4	15.9	17.5	16.9	14.5
Manufactures	52.6	51.9	46.0	49.6	63.4	69.6	73.7	72.5	73.3	74.2
Chemicals	9.2	10.0	9.9	10.2	11.3	10.5	9.8	9.2	9.1	9.0
Goods classified chiefly by material	13.3	12.4	12.0	14.5	17.7	19.2	19.2	19.8	19.6	19.5
Machinery and transport equipment	26.4	26.1	21.1	21.6	29.3	33.9	38.3	36.8	36.9	36.5
Miscellaneous	3.6	3.4	3.0	3.3	5.1	6.1	6.3	6.7	7.7	9.2
Unspecified	0.2	0.3	0.2	0.3	0.6	0.3	0.1	0.1	0.1	0.1
Exports, total (Million $)	4 173.3	4 601.4	5 207.5	5 685.4	7 204.9	9 318.3	10 989.7	12 797.7	16 415.7	16 326.1
As a percentage of total										
Food and beverages	9.7	9.6	8.8	7.8	8.2	7.3	7.7	7.0	6.6	7.3
Basic material and semi-finished goods	15.2	15.6	15.2	14.5	12.2	11.9	12.8	14.0	12.8	10.5
Manufactures	73.3	72.6	75.3	76.0	78.4	80.1	79.1	78.6	80.3	81.9
Chemicals	8.2	7.5	7.7	7.0	6.1	5.4	6.0	5.6	5.2	4.6
Goods classified chiefly by material	29.9	28.7	28.1	27.7	26.4	25.4	25.4	23.7	23.4	24.1
Machinery and transport equipment	14.0	15.4	17.3	15.6	15.7	16.5	16.7	19.1	19.6	19.7
Miscellaneous	21.1	21.0	22.2	25.7	30.3	32.8	31.0	30.3	32.1	33.6
Unspecified	1.8	2.2	0.8	1.7	1.2	0.7	0.4	0.4	0.3	0.3

Source: OECD, Foreign Trade Statistics, Series C.

Table I. Geographical breakdown of foreign trade

Billion escudos and percentages

	1982	1983	1984	1985	1986	1987	1988	1989	1990	1991
Exports, total (Billion escudos)	356.7	538.0	796.6	951.0	1 055.5	1 304.8	1 598.8	2 037.1	2 256.9	2 420.7
As a percentage of total										
OECD countries	82.0	82.8	84.1	85.4	89.1	91.0	90.6	90.7	91.2	91.0
EC	61.0	63.1	62.1	62.6	68.3	71.1	72.0	71.8	73.9	75.4
Germany	13.1	13.6	13.8	13.8	14.7	15.4	14.7	15.7	16.7	19.2
France	13.1	13.7	12.5	12.7	15.2	15.8	15.2	15.0	15.5	14.4
Italy	4.8	4.1	4.3	4.0	3.9	3.9	4.2	4.3	4.1	4.0
United Kingdom	14.8	14.7	15.4	14.6	14.2	14.1	14.3	12.3	12.1	10.8
Spain	3.6	4.1	4.4	4.2	6.9	9.3	11.5	12.7	13.5	15.1
Other EC	11.5	13.0	11.7	13.4	13.3	12.6	12.1	11.8	11.9	11.9
United States	6.1	6.0	8.8	9.2	7.0	6.4	5.9	5.9	4.8	3.8
Other OECD countries	14.9	13.7	13.1	13.6	13.8	13.5	12.6	12.9	12.5	11.7
Non OECD countries	15.9	15.5	14.5	13.3	10.0	8.2	8.1	8.3	7.8	8.0
of which: OPEC	2.9	3.6	2.5	2.5	1.6	1.5	1.1	0.7	0.6	0.5
Previous Escudo Area	4.9	4.5	4.4	3.9	2.1	2.1	2.7	3.3	3.4	4.1
Imports, total (Billion escudos)	809.0	949.2	1 195.0	1 282.0	1 400.1	1 956.0	2 597.8	3 035.8	3 469.6	3 906.1
As a percentage of total										
OECD countries	69.3	69.8	66.7	67.1	78.4	81.7	84.0	83.5	83.4	85.5
EC	46.7	44.9	43.3	46.1	58.9	63.8	67.3	68.2	69.2	72.0
Germany	11.9	11.5	10.2	11.7	14.4	15.1	14.7	14.6	14.4	15.0
France	8.6	8.1	7.9	8.0	10.0	11.2	11.5	11.7	11.5	12.0
Italy	5.5	5.1	4.7	5.1	7.9	8.7	9.3	9.1	10.0	10.2
United Kingdom	7.7	7.7	6.8	7.5	7.5	8.1	8.3	7.5	7.6	7.5
Spain	6.1	5.2	7.1	7.4	11.0	11.7	13.2	14.5	14.4	15.8
Other EC	6.9	7.3	6.4	6.3	8.2	8.9	10.3	10.8	11.3	11.5
United States	10.8	14.3	13.6	9.7	7.0	4.8	4.3	4.4	3.9	3.4
Other OECD countries	11.8	10.6	9.8	11.3	12.4	13.0	12.5	10.8	10.3	10.1
Non OECD countries	30.3	29.7	32.8	32.0	21.2	18.2	15.9	16.5	16.6	14.5
of which: OPEC	19.5	18.6	18.9	17.6	8.5	6.0	4.9	6.1	6.7	4.7
Previous Escudo Area	0.4	0.4	0.7	1.2	0.8	0.4	0.2	0.4	0.4	0.5

Source: INE, *Boletim mensal das estatísticas do comercio externo.*

Table J. Balance of payments

Million US dollars

	1982	1983	1984	1985	1986	1987	1988	1989	1990	1991
Exports, fob	4 108	4 569	5 177	5 673	7 202	9 268	10 875	12 716	16 301	16 223
Imports, fob	8 941	7 643	7 307	7 177	8 882	12 849	16 393	17 594	23 129	24 078
Trade balance	-4 833	-3 074	-2 130	-1 504	-1 680	-3 581	-5 518	-4 878	-6 828	-7 855
Services, net	-1 092	-742	-674	-361	-85	250	137	478	1 147	1 151
Travel	609	588	728	901	1 203	1 721	1 869	2 102	2 688	2 686
Transportation	-282	-200	-192	-184	-135	-373	-587	-663	-889	-1 023
Investment income	-1 269	-1 066	-1 202	-1 152	-1 014	-932	-877	-718	-233	82
Government transactions	-65	-37	-40	-44	-56	-123	-131	-135	-162	-182
Other services	-85	-27	32	118	-83	-43	-137	-108	-257	-412
Transfers, net	2 680	2 171	2 179	2 251	2 915	3 775	4 317	4 539	5 500	5 962
Current balance	-3 245	-1 645	-625	386	1 150	444	-1 064	139	-181	-742
Medium and long-term capital	2 582	1 458	1 333	1 109	-293	194	843	2 798	3 576	3 981
Private	1 946	858	835	729	-196	195	811	2 243	2 215	2 936
Official	636	600	498	380	-97	-1	32	555	1 361	1 045
Short-term and unrecorded	786	-564	-221	-523	-1 079	1 273	1 826	993	553	1 766
Non-monetary transactions, net	123	-751	487	972	-222	1 911	1 605	3 930	3 948	5 005
Private monetary institutions short-term capital	-15	-310	-289	4	199	-101	-671	633	-446	771
Balance on official settlements	108	-1 061	198	976	-23	1 810	934	4 563	3 502	5 776
Use of IMF credit	-43	366	221	0	0	0	0	0	0	0
Miscellaneous official accounts	-103	0	-287	-284	-82	-309	-556	92	26	-87
Changes in reserves (increase = –)	38	695	-132	-692	105	-1 501	-378	-4 655	-3 528	-5 689

Source: Bank of Portugal.

Table K. **Labour-market indicators**

A. LABOUR MARKET PERFORMANCE

	Cyclical Peak: 1979	Cyclical Trough: 1984	1985	1991
Standardised unemployment rate	..	8.4	8.5	4.1
Unemployment rate: Total	7.5	8.1	8.1	4.0
Male	4.0	5.7	6.1	2.7
Women	12.5	11.3	11.0	5.8
Youth[2]	17.8	19.6	19.5	9.1
Share of long-term unemployment in total unemployment[3]	..	43.6	48.4	30.2

B. STRUCTURAL OR INSTITUTIONAL CHARACTERISTICS

	1975	1980	1985	1991[1]
Participation rate[4]: Total	70.7	71.8	71.8	74.0
Male	93.3	90.8	85.8	85.5
Women	50.6	54.9	58.8	63.2
Employment/population (15-64 years)	64.3	65.0	65.5	70.9
Non-wage labour costs[5] (as a percentage of total compensation)	13.4	14.5	18.4	20.2
Unemployment insurance replacement ratio[6]	..	32.4	28.8	26.8
Minimum wage, non-agricultural sector (workers of 20 years and more, as a percentage of the average earnings)	..	..	..	44.7

Average percentage changes (annual rates)	1970/1960	1980/1970	1985/1980	1991/1986
Labour force	0.5	2.0	0.7	1.5
Employment: Total	0.4	1.4	0.5	2.5
Industries	0.7	2.7	–0.9	2.4
Services	4.3	1.4	3.8	4.7

1. Non-wage labour costs : 1990.
2. People between 15 and 24 years as a percentage of the labour force of the same age group.
3. Persons seeking a job for 12 months and over as a percentage of total unemployed.
4. Labour force as a percentage of relevant population group, aged between 15 and 64 years.
5. Employers' contributions to social security and pension funds.
6. Unemployment benefits per unemployed as a percentage of compensation per employee.
Source: OECD, *Labour Force Statistics.*

Table L. **Public sector**

A. BUDGET INDICATORS : GENERAL GOVERNMENT ACCOUNT
Per cent of GDP[1]

	1970	1980	1985	1991
Current receipts	29.6	31.4	36.0	38.5
Non-interest expenditure	29.0	22.8	34.0	36.9
Primary budget balance	0.5	8.6	1.9	1.6
Interest payments	0.5	3.1	9.3	8.4
General government budget balance	1.5	5.5	−7.4	−6.8

B. THE STRUCTURE OF EXPENDITURE AND TAXATION
Per cent of GDP
1. Structure of general government expenditure

		1970	1980	1985	1991
Total expenditure		29.6	25.9	43.4	45.4
Of which:	Current consumption	14.2	14.5	15.5	17.6
	Transfers to persons	4.2	10.9	11.0	14.4
	Subsidies	1.5	5.2	3.6	1.2
	Capital formation	2.5	4.1	3.1	3.6
Expenditure by fonction:	Education	..	3.4	3.8	..
	Health	..	2.6	3.5	..
	Pensions	..	0.9	0.7	..

2. Structure of taxation[2]

	Portugal		EC	
	1980	1990	1980	1990
Total tax revenue	28.7	34.6	36.9	40.8
Income tax	5.7	8.8	12.7	14.1
Social security	8.5	9.6	10.7	11.5
Consumption tax	12.9	15.2	11.3	12.8

1. On a national accounts basis.
2. On the basis of revenue statistics which may be different from National Accounts.
Sources: OECD, National Accounts; Revenue Statistics of OECD Member Countries.

Table M. **Production and employment structures**

	Per cent share of GDP at factor cost (current prices)				Per cent share of total employment			
	1977	1980	1985	1990	1977	1980	1985	1990
Agriculture, forestry and fishing	11.9	10.3	8.0	5.8	31.8	27.2	25.4	20.3
Manufacturing	27.9	31.0	30.4	27.9	23.6	25.1	24.3	23.8
Of which: Food, forestry and tobacco	5.7	5.7	6.1	6.0	3.5	3.3	3.2	3.3
Textiles, clothing, leather	5.4	7.0	7.8	7.2	7.6	8.1	8.3	8.3
Wood, paper and paper products	3.4	3.7	3.2	3.1	3.1	3.2	2.9	2.7
Chemicals and products of petroleum, coal, rubber, etc.	3.0	2.8	3.3	2.1	1.5	1.7	1.6	1.5
Non-mineral products except products of petroleum and coal	2.4	2.6	2.1	1.9	1.8	1.9	1.7	1.7
Fabricated metal products, machinery and equipment	5.6	6.8	5.6	4.9	4.0	4.5	4.2	3.9
Electricity, gas and water	1.9	2.1	3.5	3.1	0.6	0.8	0.9	0.8
Construction	7.7	7.1	5.7	6.9	9.5	10.1	9.5	9.9
Services	50.6	49.5	52.5	56.4	34.4	36.8	39.9	45.2
Of which: Wholesale and retail trade, restaurants, and hotels	21.4	21.7	22.4	19.8	13.0	13.4	13.6	17.2
Transportation, storage and communication	5.6	5.5	7.7	5.4	4.6	4.5	4.4	4.4
Finance, insurance, real estate and business services	10.7	10.5	10.1	13.1	2.2	2.6	3.0	3.2

Source: OECD, *National Accounts.*

BASIC STATISTICS:

INTERNATIONAL COMPARISONS

	Units	Reference period[1]	Australia	Austria	Belgium	Canada
Population						
Total	Thousands	1990	17 085	7 718	9 967	26 620
Inhabitants per sq. km	Number	1990	2	92	327	3
Net average annual increase over previous 10 years . .	%	1990	1.5	0.2	0.1	1
Employment						
Total civilian employment (TCE)[2]	Thousands	1990	7 850	3 412	3 726	12 572
Of which : Agriculture...................	% of TCE		5.6	7.9	2.7	4.2
Industry	% of TCE		25.4	36.8	28.3	24.6
Services	% of TCE		69	55.3	69	71.2
Gross domestic product (GDP)						
At current prices and current exchange rates	Bill US $	1990	294.1	157.4	192.4	570.1
Per capita	US $		17 215	20 391	19 303	21 418
At current prices using current PPP's[3]	Bill US $	1990	271.7	127.4	163	510.5
Per capita	US $		15 900	16 513	16 351	19 179
Average annual volume growth over previous 5 years .	%	1990	3.1	3.1	3.2	3
Gross fixed capital formation (GFCF)	% of GDP	1990	22.9	24.3	20.3	21.4
Of which: Machinery and equipment	% of GDP		9.7	10.1	10.4	7.2
Residential construction	% of GDP	1990	4.8	4.6	4.3	6.8
Average annual volume growth over previous 5 years .	%	1990	2.4	4.6	9.5	5.8
Gross saving ratio[4]	% of GDP	1990	19.7	26	21.8	17.4
General government						
Current expenditure on goods and services	% of GDP	1990	17.3	18	14.3	19.8
Current disbursements[5]	% of GDP	1990	34.9	44.9	53.1	44
Current receipts	% of GDP	1990	35.1	46.7	49.5	41.6
Net official development assistance	Mill US $	1990	0.34	0.25	0.45	0.44
Indicators of living standards						
Private consumption per capita using current PPP's[3]	US $	1990	9 441	9 154	10 119	11 323
Passenger cars per 1 000 inhabitants	Number	1989	570	416	416	613
Telephones per 1 000 inhabitants	Number	1989	550 (85)	540	500 (88)	780
Television sets per 1 000 inhabitants	Number	1988	217	484 (89)	255	586
Doctors per 1 000 inhabitants	Number	1990	2.3	2.1	3.4	2.2
Infant mortality per 1 000 live births	Number	1990	8.2	7.8	7.9	7.2
Wages and prices (average annual increase over **previous 5 years)**						
Wages (earnings or rates according to availability) . . .	%	1990	5.6	5	3	4.3
Consumer prices	%	1990	7.9	2.2	2.1	4.5
Foreign trade						
Exports of goods, fob*	Mill US $	1990	39 813	40 985	118 291[7]	127 334
As % of GDP	%		13.5	26	61.5	22.3
Average annual increase over previous 5 years ...	%		11.9	19.1	17.1	7.8
Imports of goods, cif*	Mill US $	1990	38 907	48 914	120 330[7]	116 561
As % of GDP	%		13.2	31.1	62.5	20.4
Average annual increase over previous 5 years ...	%		11	18.6	16.5	8.8
Total official reserves[6]	Mill SDR's	1990	11 432	6 591	8 541[7]	12 544
As ratio of average monthly imports of goods	ratio		3.5	1.6	0.9	1.3

* At current prices and exchange rates.
1. Unless otherwise stated.
2. According to the definitions used in OECD Labour Force Statistics.
3. PPP's = Purchasing Power Parities.
4. Gross saving = Gross national disposable income minus Private and Government consumption.
5. Current disbursements = Current expenditure on goods and services plus current transfers and payments of property income.
6. Gold included in reserves is valued at 35 SDR's per ounce. End of year.
7. Including Luxembourg.
8. Included in Belgium.

BASIC STATISTICS: INTERNATIONAL COMPARISONS

Denmark	Finland	France	Germany	Greece	Iceland	Ireland	Italy	Japan	Luxembourg	Netherlands	New Zealand	Norway	Portugal	Spain	Sweden	Switzerland	Turkey	United Kingdom	United States
5 141	4 986	56 420	63 232	10 140	255	3 503	57 647	123 540	382	14 951	3 379	4 241	9 859	38 959	8 559	6 796	56 473	57 411	251 523
119	15	103	254	77	2	50	191	327	147	366	13	13	107	77	19	165	72	235	27
0	0.4	0.5	0.3	0.5	1.1	0.3	0.2	0.6	0.5	0.6	0.7	0.4	0	0.4	0.3	0.6	2.4	0.2	1
2 638	2 457	21 732	27 946	3 677	126	1 115	21 123	62 500	189	6 268	1 472	1992	4 474	12 578	4 508	3 563	19 209	26 577	117 914
5.6	8.4	6.1	3.4	24.5	10.3	15	9	7.2	3.2	4.6	10.6	6.5	17.8	11.8	3.3	5.6	47.8	2.1	2.8
27.5	31	29.9	39.8	27.4	30.2	28.6	32.4	34.1	30.7	26.3	24.6	24.8	34.8	33.4	29.1	35	19.9	29	26.2
66.9	60.6	64	56.8	48.2	59.5	56.4	58.6	58.7	66.1	69.1	64.8	68.8	47.4	54.8	67.5	59.5	32.3	68.9	70.9
129.3	137.3	1 190.8	1 488.2	66	5.9	42.5	1 090.8	2 940.4	8.7	279.1	44	105.7	59.7	491.2	228.1	224.8	108.4	975.1	5 392.2
5 150	27 527	21 105	23 536	6 505	22 907	12 131	18 921	23 801	22 895	18 676	13 020	24 924	6 085	12 609	26 652	33 085	1 896	16 985	21 449
85.2	82.2	980.4	1 151.6	74.3	4.1	37.2	919.7	2 179.9	7.3	234.8	45.8	68	82	457.3	144.6	142.1	189.7	911.8	5 392.2
5 570	16 487	17 376	18 212	7 323	16 158	10 627	15 953	17 645	19 282	15 708	13 564	16 033	8 364	11 738	16 896	20 911	3 318	15 882	21 449
1.5	3.4	2.9	3.1	1.7	2.7	4.4	3	4.6	4.3	2.7	0.4	1.6	4.6	4.5	2.1	2.8	5.9	3.2	3
17.7	26.3	21.2	21.2	19.7	19.4	19.1	20.2	32.2	25.3	21.5	19.8	18.8	26.4	24.6	20.7	27.1	22.7	19.2	16.1
8.1	10	9.7	9.8	8.7	6.2	9.3	10	13.7	11	10.7	9.9	6.8	13.1	8.1	8.9	9.1	11.7 (87)	8.5	7.8 (89)
3.7	7.1	5.2	5.6	5	4.4	4.2	5.2	6.1	5	5.1	4.8	2.8	4.5	5	5.5	17.9⁹	5.8 (87)	3.4	4.4 (89)
0.8	4.8	5.8	5.2	2.3	2.1	4.4	4.3	9	11.7	5.1	2.7	-2.8	10.4	11.7	4.9	6	4.7	5.8	2.7
18	23.1	21	25.2	13.8	16	23.4	19.3	34.6	60.9	25.4	16.1	24.1	26.6	22.1	17.3	33	22.2	15.6	14.4
25.2	21.1	18	18.4	21.2	18.8	15.7	17.3	9.1	16.3	14.8	16.7	21	16.7	15.2	27.1	13.3	19.4	19.9	18.1
56.5	37.5	46.2	42.6	50.9	31.5	49.9 (87)	48.1	26.2	45 (86)	51.7	..	51.6	39.3	35.5 (88)	59.1	30.7	..	38.1	34.6 (89)
56.1	41.2	46.5	43.4	34.7	34.9	43.7 (87)	42.1	34.6	52.9 (86)	49.5	..	56.2	37.6	36.3 (88)	63.9	34.2	..	40	31.8 (89)
0.93	0.64	0.79	0.42	0.07	0.03	0.16	0.32	0.31	0.29	0.94	0.22	1.17	0.23	0.16	0.9	0.31	..	0.27	0.21
3 639	8 602	10 482	9 841	5 298	9 824	5 886	9 866	10 122	11 017	9 241	8 475	8 174	5 278	7 326	8 748	11 933	1992	10 051	14 465
370	439	494	526	234	488 (85)	278	458	455	546	399	549	459	181	347	462	479	37	449	748
880 (88)	620 (85)	610 (85)	680 (88)	360 (88)	525 (83)	265 (85)	510 (88)	555 (85)	413 (85)	660 (88)	720 (88)	622 (84)	220 (88)	396 (87)	889 (83)	880 (88)	120 (88)	524 (84)	650 (84)
526	486	399	379	175	306	260	419	589	250	478	296	350	160	380	395	408	172	435	812
2.7 (87)	1.9	2.6 (89)	3 (89)	3.3 (89)	2.8 (89)	1.5 (88)	1.3 (89)	1.6 (88)	1.9 (88)	2.5	1.9 (89)	3.1	2.9	3.7 (89)	3.1 (89)	2.9 (89)	0.9	1.4 (89)	2.3
7.5 (89)	6.1 (89)	7.2	7.5 (89)	9.1 (89)	5.9	7.6 (89)	8.5	4.6 (89)	9.9	6.9	8.3	7.9 (89)	11	7.8 (89)	5.9	7.3	6.5 (89)	7.9	9.2
6	8.2	3.7	4.2	16	..	5.6	6.1	3.7	..	1.7	8.1	8.7	..	8.2	8.2	..	..	8.5	2.6
3.9	5	3.1	1.4	17.4	20.2	3.3	5.7	1.3	1.7	0.7	9.4	6.2	11.3	6.5	6.2	2.5	53.7	5.9	4
4 988	26 583	216 157	409 620	8 014	1 589	23 796	170 330	287 358	..⁸	131 778	9 533	33 905	16 338	55 289	57 422	63 847	12 836	185 710	393 812
27.1	19.4	18.2	27.5	12.2	27.1	56	15.6	9.8	..	47.2	21.7	32.1	27.4	11.3	25.2	28.4	11.8	19	7.3
15.6	14.3	16.5	17.6	11.8	14.2	18.1	16.6	10.2	..	14	10.6	11.2	23.5	18	13.7	18.4	9.9	12.9	13.1
4 647	26 950	225 260	344 454	19 831	1 648	20 687	181 863	235 407	..	126 215	9 458	27 218	24 874	87 373	54 659	69 811	22 224	225 327	494 842
24.5	19.6	18.9	23.1	30.1	28.1	48.7	16.7	16.7	..	45.2	21.5	25.7	41.7	17.8	24	31	20.5	23.1	9.2
11.8	15.3	16.8	16.9	14.1	12.7	15.7	14.8	12.6	..	14.1	9.6	11.9	26.5	24	14	17.8	14.2	15.5	7.4
7 445	6 779	25 851	47 729	2 398	307	3 672	44 232	55 179	..	12 289	2 902	10 777	10 182	36 008	12 644	20 541	4 252	25 201	50 791
2.8	3	1.4	1.7	1.5	2.2	2.1	2.9	2.8	..	1.2	3.7	4.8	4.9	4.9	2.8	3.5	2.3	1.3	1.2

ncluding non-residential construction.
ederal Government Statistics.

ces: Population and Employment: OECD Labour Force Statistics.
    GDP, GFCF, and General Government: OECD National Accounts, Vol. I and OECD Economic Outlook, Historical Statistics.
    Indicators of living standards: Miscellaneous national publications.
    Wages and Prices: OECD Main Economic Indicators.
    Foreign trade: OECD Monthly Foreign Trade Statistics, series A.
    Total official reserves: IMF International Financial Statistics.

EMPLOYMENT OPPORTUNITIES

Economics Department, OECD

The Economics Department of the OECD offers challenging and rewarding opportunities to economists interested in applied policy analysis in an international environment. The Department's concerns extend across the entire field of economic policy analysis, both macro-economic and micro-economic. Its main task is to provide, for discussion by committees of senior officials from Member countries, documents and papers dealing with current policy concerns. Within this programme of work, three major responsibilities are:

- to prepare regular surveys of the economies of individual Member countries;
- to issue full twice-yearly reviews of the economic situation and prospects of the OECD countries in the context of world economic trends;
- to analyse specific policy issues in a medium-term context for theOECD as a whole, and to a lesser extent for the non-OECD countries.

The documents prepared for these purposes, together with much of the Department's other economic work, appear in published form in the *OECD Economic Outlook, OECD Economic Surveys, OECD Economic Studies* and the Department's *Working Papers* series.

The Department maintains a world econometric model, INTERLINK, which plays an important role in the preparation of the policy analyses and twice-yearly projections. The availability of extensive cross-country data bases and good computer resources facilitates comparative empirical analysis, much of which is incorporated into the model.

The Department is made up of about 75 professional economists from a variety of backgrounds and Member countries. Most projects are carried out by small teams and last from four to eighteen months. Within the Department, ideas and points of view are widely discussed; there is a lively professional interchange, and all professional staff have the opportunity to contribute actively to the programme of work.

Skills the Economics Department is looking for:

a) Solid competence in using the tools of both micro-economic and macro-economic theory to answer policy questions. Experience indicates that this normally requires the equivalent of a PH.D. in economics or substantial relevant professional experience to compensate for a lower degree.

b) Solid knowledge of economic statistics and quantitative methods; this includes how to identify data, estimate structural relationships, apply basic techniques of time series analysis, and test hypotheses. It is essential to be able to interpret results sensibly in an economic policy context.

c) A keen interest in and knowledge of policy issues, economic developments and their political/social contexts.

d) Interest and experience in analysing questions posed by policy-makers and presenting the results to them effectively and judiciously. Thus, work experience in government agencies or policy research institutions is an advantage.

e) The ability to write clearly, effectively, and to the point. The OECD is a bilingual organisation with French and English as the official languages. Candidates must have excellent knowledge of one of these languages, and some knowledge of the other. Knowledge of other languages might also be an advantage for certain posts.

f) For some posts, expertise in a particular area may be important, but a successful candidate is expected to be able to work on a broader range of topics relevant to the work of the Department. Thus, except in rare cases, the Department does not recruit narrow specialists.

g) The Department works on a tight time schedule and strict deadlines. Moreover, much of the work in the Department is carried out in small groups of economists. Thus, the ability to work with other economists from a variety of cultural and professional backgrounds, to supervise junior staff, and to produce work on time is important.

General Information

The salary for recruits depends on educational and professional background. Positions carry a basic salary from FF 262 512 or FF 323 916 for Administrators (economists) and from FF 375 708 for Principal Administrators (senior economists). This may be supplemented by expatriation and/or family allowances, depending on nationality, residence and family situation. Initial appointments are for a fixed term of two to three years.

Vacancies are open to candidates from OECD Member countries. The Organisation seeks to maintain an appropriate balance between female and male staff and among nationals from Member countries.

For further information on employment opportunities in the Economics Department, contact:

Administrative Unit
Economics Department
OECD
2, rue André-Pascal
75775 PARIS CEDEX 16
FRANCE

Applications citing "ECSUR", together with a detailed *curriculum vitae* in English or French, should be sent to the Head of Personnel at the above address.

MAIN SALES OUTLETS OF OECD PUBLICATIONS
PRINCIPAUX POINTS DE VENTE DES PUBLICATIONS DE L'OCDE

ARGENTINA – ARGENTINE
Carlos Hirsch S.R.L.
Galería Güemes, Florida 165, 4° Piso
1333 Buenos Aires   Tel. (1) 331.1787 y 331.2391
                    Telefax: (1) 331.1787

AUSTRALIA – AUSTRALIE
D.A. Information Services
648 Whitehorse Road, P.O.B 163
Mitcham, Victoria 3132   Tel. (03) 873.4411
                    Telefax: (03) 873.5679

AUSTRIA – AUTRICHE
Gerold & Co.
Graben 31
Wien I   Tel. (0222) 533.50.14

BELGIUM – BELGIQUE
Jean De Lannoy
Avenue du Roi 202
B-1060 Bruxelles   Tel. (02) 538.51.69/538.08.41
                    Telefax: (02) 538.08.41

CANADA
Renouf Publishing Company Ltd.
1294 Algoma Road
Ottawa, ON K1B 3W8   Tel. (613) 741.4333
                    Telefax: (613) 741.5439
Stores:
61 Sparks Street
Ottawa, ON K1P 5R1   Tel. (613) 238.8985
211 Yonge Street
Toronto, ON M5B 1M4   Tel. (416) 363.3171
                    Telefax: (416)363.59.63

Les Éditions La Liberté Inc.
3020 Chemin Sainte-Foy
Sainte-Foy, PQ G1X 3V6   Tel. (418) 658.3763
                    Telefax: (418) 658.3763

Federal Publications
165 University Avenue
Toronto, ON M5H 3B8   Tel. (416) 581.1552
                    Telefax: (416) 581.1743

Les Publications Fédérales
1185 Avenue de l'Université
Montréal, PQ H3B 3A7   Tel. (514) 954.1633
                    Telefax : (514) 954.1633

CHINA – CHINE
China National Publications Import
Export Corporation (CNPIEC)
16 Gongti E. Road, Chaoyang District
P.O. Box 88 or 50
Beijing 100704 PR   Tel. (01) 506.6688
                    Telefax: (01) 506.3101

DENMARK – DANEMARK
Munksgaard Export and Subscription Service
35, Nørre Søgade, P.O. Box 2148
DK-1016 København K   Tel. (33) 12.85.70
                    Telefax: (33) 12.93.87

FINLAND – FINLANDE
Akateeminen Kirjakauppa
Keskuskatu 1, P.O. Box 128
00100 Helsinki   Tel. (358 0) 12141
                    Telefax: (358 0) 121.4441

FRANCE
OECD/OCDE
Mail Orders/Commandes par correspondance:
2, rue André-Pascal
75775 Paris Cedex 16   Tel. (33-1) 45.24.82.00
Telefax: (33-1) 45.24.81.76   or (33-1) 45.24.85.00
                    Telex: 640048 OCDE

OECD Bookshop/Librairie de l'OCDE :
33, rue Octave-Feuillet
75016 Paris   Tel. (33-1) 45.24.81.67
                    (33-1) 45.24.81.81

Documentation Française
29, quai Voltaire
75007 Paris   Tel. 40.15.70.00
Gibert Jeune (Droit-Économie)
6, place Saint-Michel
75006 Paris   Tel. 43.25.91.19
Librairie du Commerce International
10, avenue d'Iéna
75016 Paris   Tel. 40.73.34.60
Librairie Dunod
Université Paris-Dauphine
Place du Maréchal de Lattre de Tassigny
75016 Paris   Tel. 47.27.18.56
Librairie Lavoisier
11, rue Lavoisier
75008 Paris   Tel. 42.65.39.95
Librairie L.G.D.J. - Montchrestien
20, rue Soufflot
75005 Paris   Tel. 46.33.89.85
Librairie des Sciences Politiques
30, rue Saint-Guillaume
75007 Paris   Tel. 45.48.36.02
P.U.F.
49, boulevard Saint-Michel
75005 Paris   Tel. 43.25.83.40
Librairie de l'Université
12a, rue Nazareth
13100 Aix-en-Provence   Tel. (16) 42.26.18.08
Documentation Française
165, rue Garibaldi
69003 Lyon   Tel. (16) 78.63.32.23
Librairie Decitre
29, place Bellecour
69002 Lyon   Tel. (16) 72.40.54.54

GERMANY – ALLEMAGNE
OECD Publications and Information Centre
August-Bebel-Allee 6
D-W 5300 Bonn 2   Tel. (0228) 959.120
                    Telefax: (0228) 959.12.17

GREECE – GRÈCE
Librairie Kauffmann
Mavrokordatou 9
106 78 Athens   Tel. 322.21.60
                    Telefax: 363.39.67

HONG-KONG
Swindon Book Co. Ltd.
13–15 Lock Road
Kowloon, Hong Kong   Tel. 366.80.31
                    Telefax: 739.49.75

HUNGARY – HONGRIE
Euro Info Service
POB 1271
1464 Budapest   Tel. (1) 111.62.16
                    Telefax : (1) 111.60.61

ICELAND – ISLANDE
Mál Mog Menning
Laugavegi 18, Pósthólf 392
121 Reykjavik   Tel. 162.35.23

INDIA – INDE
Oxford Book and Stationery Co.
Scindia House
New Delhi 110001   Tel.(11) 331.5896/5308
                    Telefax: (11) 332.5993
17 Park Street
Calcutta 700016   Tel. 240832

INDONESIA – INDONÉSIE
Pdii-Lipi
P.O. Box 269/JKSMG/88
Jakarta 12790   Tel. 583467
                    Telex: 62 875

IRELAND – IRLANDE
TDC Publishers – Library Suppliers
12 North Frederick Street
Dublin 1   Tel. 74.48.35/74.96.77
                    Telefax: 74.84.16

ISRAEL
Electronic Publications only
Publications électroniques seulement
Sophist Systems Ltd.
71 Allenby Street
Tel-Aviv 65134   Tel. 3-29.00.21
                    Telefax: 3-29.92.39

ITALY – ITALIE
Libreria Commissionaria Sansoni
Via Duca di Calabria 1/1
50125 Firenze   Tel. (055) 64.54.15
                    Telefax: (055) 64.12.57
Via Bartolini 29
20155 Milano   Tel. (02) 36.50.83
Editrice e Libreria Herder
Piazza Montecitorio 120
00186 Roma   Tel. 679.46.28
                    Telefax: 678.47.51
Libreria Hoepli
Via Hoepli 5
20121 Milano   Tel. (02) 86.54.46
                    Telefax: (02) 805.28.86
Libreria Scientifica
Dott. Lucio de Biasio 'Aeiou'
Via Coronelli, 6
20146 Milano   Tel. (02) 48.95.45.52
                    Telefax: (02) 48.95.45.48

JAPAN – JAPON
OECD Publications and Information Centre
Landic Akasaka Building
2-3-4 Akasaka, Minato-ku
Tokyo 107   Tel. (81.3) 3586.2016
                    Telefax: (81.3) 3584.7929

KOREA – CORÉE
Kyobo Book Centre Co. Ltd.
P.O. Box 1658, Kwang Hwa Moon
Seoul   Tel. 730.78.91
                    Telefax: 735.00.30

MALAYSIA – MALAISIE
Co-operative Bookshop Ltd.
University of Malaya
P.O. Box 1127, Jalan Pantai Baru
59700 Kuala Lumpur
Malaysia   Tel. 756.5000/756.5425
                    Telefax: 757.3661

MEXICO – MEXIQUE
Revistas y Periodicos Internacionales S.A. de C.V.
Florencia 57 - 1004
Mexico, D.F. 06600   Tel. 207.81.00
                    Telefax : 208.39.79

NETHERLANDS – PAYS-BAS
SDU Uitgeverij
Christoffel Plantijnstraat 2
Postbus 20014
2500 EA's-Gravenhage   Tel. (070 3) 78.99.11
Voor bestellingen: Tel. (070 3) 78.98.80
                    Telefax: (070 3) 47.63.51

NEW ZEALAND
NOUVELLE-ZÉLANDE
Legislation Services
P.O. Box 12418
Thorndon, Wellington   Tel. (04) 496.5652
                    Telefax: (04) 496.5698

NORWAY – NORVÈGE
Narvesen Info Center – NIC
Bertrand Narvesens vei 2
P.O. Box 6125 Etterstad
0602 Oslo 6   Tel. (02) 57.33.00
                               Telefax: (02) 68.19.01

PAKISTAN
Mirza Book Agency
65 Shahrah Quaid-E-Azam
Lahore 54000   Tel. (42) 353.601
                               Telefax: (42) 231.730

PHILIPPINE – PHILIPPINES
International Book Center
5th Floor, Filipinas Life Bldg.
Ayala Avenue
Metro Manila   Tel. 81.96.76
                               Telex 23312 RHP PH

PORTUGAL
Livraria Portugal
Rua do Carmo 70-74
Apart. 2681
1117 Lisboa Codex   Tel.: (01) 347.49.82/3/4/5
                        Telefax: (01) 347.02.64

SINGAPORE – SINGAPOUR
Information Publications Pte. Ltd.
41, Kallang Pudding, No. 04-03
Singapore 1334   Tel. 741.5166
                               Telefax: 742.9356

SPAIN – ESPAGNE
Mundi-Prensa Libros S.A.
Castelló 37, Apartado 1223
Madrid 28001   Tel. (91) 431.33.99
                               Telefax: (91) 575.39.98

Libreria Internacional AEDOS
Consejo de Ciento 391
08009 – Barcelona   Tel. (93) 488.34.92
                               Telefax: (93) 487.76.59
Llibreria de la Generalitat
Palau Moja
Rambla dels Estudis, 118
08002 – Barcelona
            (Subscripcions) Tel. (93) 318.80.12
            (Publicacions) Tel. (93) 302.67.23
                        Telefax: (93) 412.18.54

SRI LANKA
Centre for Policy Research
c/o Colombo Agencies Ltd.
No. 300-304, Galle Road
Colombo 3   Tel. (1) 574240, 573551-2
                        Telefax: (1) 575394, 510711

SWEDEN – SUÈDE
Fritzes Fackboksföretaget
Box 16356
Regeringsgatan 12
103 27 Stockholm   Tel. (08) 690.90.90
                               Telefax: (08) 20.50.21
Subscription Agency-Agence d'abonnements
Wennergren-Williams AB
P.O. Box 1305
171 25 Solna   Tel. (08) 705.97.50
                               Téléfax : (08) 27.00.71

SWITZERLAND – SUISSE
Maditec S.A. (Books and Periodicals - Livres
et périodiques)
Chemin des Palettes 4
Case postale 2066
1020 Renens 1   Tel. (021) 635.08.65
                               Telefax: (021) 635.07.80

Librairie Payot S.A.
4, place Pépinet
1003 Lausanne   Tel. (021) 341.33.48
                               Telefax: (021) 341.33.45

Librairie Unilivres
6, rue de Candolle
1205 Genève   Tel. (022) 320.26.23
                               Telefax: (022) 329.73.18

Subscription Agency - Agence d'abonnement
Dynapresse Marketing S.A.
38 avenue Vibert
1227 Carouge   Tel.: (022) 308.07.89
                               Telefax : (022) 308.07.99

See also – Voir aussi :
OECD Publications and Information Centre
August-Bebel-Allee 6
D-W 5300 Bonn 2 (Germany) Tel. (0228) 959.120
                               Telefax: (0228) 959.12.17

TAIWAN – FORMOSE
Good Faith Worldwide Int'l. Co. Ltd.
9th Floor, No. 118, Sec. 2
Chung Hsiao E. Road
Taipei   Tel. (02) 391.7396/391.7397
                        Telefax: (02) 394.9176

THAILAND – THAÏLANDE
Suksit Siam Co. Ltd.
113, 115 Fuang Nakhon Rd.
Opp. Wat Rajbopith
Bangkok 10200   Tel. (662) 251.1630
                               Telefax: (662) 236.7783

TURKEY – TURQUIE
Kültür Yayinlari Is-Türk Ltd. Sti.
Atatürk Bulvari No. 191/Kat 13
Kavaklidere/Ankara   Tel. 428.11.40 Ext. 2458
Dolmabahce Cad. No. 29
Besiktas/Istanbul   Tel. 260.71.88
                               Telex: 43482B

UNITED KINGDOM – ROYAUME-UNI
HMSO
Gen. enquiries   Tel. (071) 873 0011
Postal orders only:
P.O. Box 276, London SW8 5DT
Personal Callers HMSO Bookshop
49 High Holborn, London WC1V 6HB
                               Telefax: (071) 873 8200
Branches at: Belfast, Birmingham, Bristol, Edin-
burgh, Manchester

UNITED STATES – ÉTATS-UNIS
OECD Publications and Information Centre
2001 L Street N.W., Suite 700
Washington, D.C. 20036-4910 Tel. (202) 785.6323
                               Telefax: (202) 785.0350

VENEZUELA
Libreria del Este
Avda F. Miranda 52, Aptdo. 60337
Edificio Galipán
Caracas 106   Tel. 951.1705/951.2307/951.1297
                        Telegram: Libreste Caracas

Subscription to OECD periodicals may also be
placed through main subscription agencies.

Les abonnements aux publications périodiques de
l'OCDE peuvent être souscrits auprès des
principales agences d'abonnement.

Orders and inquiries from countries where Distribu-
tors have not yet been appointed should be sent to:
OECD Publications Service, 2 rue André-Pascal,
75775 Paris Cedex 16, France.

Les commandes provenant de pays où l'OCDE n'a
pas encore désigné de distributeur devraient être
adressées à : OCDE, Service des Publications,
2, rue André-Pascal, 75775 Paris Cedex 16, France.

04-1993

PRINTED IN FRANCE

•

OECD PUBLICATIONS
2 rue André-Pascal
75775 PARIS CEDEX 16
No. 46513
(10 93 23 1) ISBN 92-64-13921-4
ISSN 0376-6438

•